ULTRA LOW CARB NUTRIBULLET RECIPE BOOK

203 NutriBullet Ultra Low Carb Delicious and Optimally Nutritious Blast and Smoothie Recipes

RECIPROCITY

Third Edition published by Reciprocity in 2015
All rights reserved

EDITOR
James Watkins

WRITERS
Marco Black and Oliver Lahoud

Copyright © Reciprocity, London 2015

All Rights Reserved. No part of this publication may be reproduced, stored in a retrieval system, or transmitted, in any form, or by any means, electronic, mechanical, photocopying, recording or otherwise, without the prior permission of the publisher and copyright holder.

Disclaimer
The information in this book is provided on the basis that neither the authors nor the editors nor the publishers shall have any responsibility for any loss or damage that results or is claimed to have resulted from reading it. Some of the recipes contain nuts or nut milk. If you have a nut allergy please avoid those particular recipes.

CONTENTS

All recipes are stated in Cups, Grams and Ounces.

The precise nutritional break down into Protein grams, Fat grams, Carb grams, Fibre grams and Kcals is calculated for each recipe using data from the U.S. Department of Agriculture database.

Mega Low Carb Smoothies
(With no more than 5 Carb Grams)

Ultra Low Carb Superfood Blasts
Made entirely out of Superfoods and Cucumber (With Carb Grams)

Ultra Low Carb Superfood Smoothies
Made entirely out of Superfoods and Cucumber (With Carb Grams)

Happiness and Deep Sleep Blasts
High in Tryptophan, Magnesium,. Vits B3, B6, B9 (With Carb Grams)

Heart Care Blasts
Anti-inflammatory, high in Omega 3, anti oxidants, Vitamins C, E (With Carb Grams)

Detoxing and Cleansing Blasts
All ingredients have detoxing capabilities (With Carb Grams)

Ultra Low Carb Double Fruit Smoothies
Carbs are the poison exercise is the antidote (With Carb Grams)

Ulra Low Carb Fruit and Veggie Blasts
Carbs are the poison exercise is the antidote (With Carb Grams)

Ultra Low Carb Fruit and Veggie Smoothies
Carbs are the poison exercise is the antidote (With Carb Grams)

The Lower the Carbs the Better the Health

The view until a few years ago was that saturated fat was bad for your heart, bad for your arteries and caused weight gain. This view was based upon the premise that "You are what you eat." So it seemed logical to believe that if you ate fat you would get fat.

However the human body is not a passive recipient of food. If you eat a hamburger you do not become a hamburger. The body metabolises everything that we eat. So we are not what we eat at all. We are, in fact, what the body makes out of what we eat. Putting this another way..

"We are what we eat – metabolised"

The supermarket shelves are full of low fat foods. These were supposed to make us all thinner. But the truth is that in the West, the average person is getting fatter not thinner. Yes fat contains 9 kcal per gram whereas protein and carbohydrate contain only 4 kcal per gram. So again it seemed logical to deduce that cutting down on fat would makes us thinner and healthier. Many people today religiously cut all the fat off their meat before consumption. It's a noble effort. But we now know, from bitter experience, that it is doomed to failure. Nature provides whole foods for a reason. And we should eat what is provided whole as much as possible. For fat is an apetite suppressor and it is not the villain of the obesity epidemic. It was merely the most obvious suspect.

Carb, carbs, carbs are the disaster. And every supermarket is full of them. Our food shops are a sea of carbohydrate. That is why we are getting fatter and fatter. And that is why 30% of people over 60 in the West are diabetic. We are overloading our carb metabolisms from day one. When you eat too much carb and do not burn it off, you stress our your pancreas and become ill. When you eat too much fat you do not. Eskimos have been eating no carbs for hundreds of years – because you cannot grow much wheat in the arctic. They used to have no diabetes at all until they started eating cookies and sitting about in front of computers rather than catching fish and building igloos.

The even more counter intuitive result of the latest dietary research is that high carb diets cause cardio vascular disease and arterial sclerosis not fats. Eating more fat and therefore less carb actually improves your blood lipids (blood fats such as cholesterol). The writer was diabetic and now eats an ultra low carb diet with an enormous amount of saturated fat. Initially he thought that this would make him into a heart attack waiting to happen. But his cholesterol levels have only improved the more fat and the less carbs that he has eaten!

So the moral of the story is that a little knowledge is a dangerous thing. Two stage thinking is what is required here not one stage thinking. Because the body is a complex and brilliant mechanism. It is not passive. It is active. If you push it in one direction, it will react and push back in the other.

FIGHT DIABETES

Ultra Low Carbs and Diabetes

To fight Type 2 successfully you have to burn off with exercise more carb grams than you ingest. That is it. I had been doing that without realising it, by keeping to a very very low carb diet and by walking a lot after meals. I started doing it religiously with a treadmill in the summer of 2013. And then in December 2013, my Doctor gave me the Christmas present that I really wanted. He pronounced me cured. My latest two HbA1c readings are 5.3% and 5.4%. I am no longer diabetic. My fasting sugar was 23.0 mmol/L or 414 mg/dl on diagnosis in November 2012.

If you have type 2 then you cannot store blood sugar as glycogen effectively. Your glucose warehouse is full up or your fork lift driver is having a tea break.

If you cannot store it then you have to stop eating it. The trouble is that the brain needs sugar or you go into a hypo. So even if you do not eat very much carb (which is long chain sugars) the liver will still manage to produce sugar for your brain from the protein you eat or actually from your own muscle if it has to.

There has recently been headline news about research into Glucokinase. This is an enzyme produce by the brain which tells the liver and the pancreas to make sugar. It is thought that reducing glucokinase could reduce the brain's addiction to sugar and help with both weight loss and diabetes. There is a real sense in which a diabetic is a sugarholic. His brain is flooding him with glucokinase. So the idea is to go cold turkey on glucose and that means going very very low carb. 50 carb grams per day maximum. Please then burn off this 50 grams of carb that you eat with at least an hour of brisk walking (at a speed where you cannot keep breathing through your nose but have to use your mouth). Then your sugar will amaze you. Diet is only half of the cure. For to a diabetic Carbs are the poison and Exercise is the antidote. And since the brain needs carbs you will always have some poison in your system. Hence an hour of brisk walking every day is needed to burn that poison up.

These recipes only use very very low carb ingredients. Loads of goodness and very very little carb is the philosophy.

The Health Benefits of NutriBullet Raw Vegetable Variation

Many clinical studies have shown that raw vegetables help fight the big killers today. They help significantly to fight Cancer (the more veggies and the less meat you eat the better your body can prevent and fight tumours). There was a wonderful study done on the Norwegians during the second world war when the German occupiers commandeered all their meat. The result was that the incidence of all types of cancer in Norwegians fell by more than 50%.

They help fight Cardio Vascular Disease. They provide essential antioxidants, oils, minerals, vitamins and are generally better for us than a hamburger or a pork sausage. But the trouble is that they normally do not taste as good as a hamburger or a pork sausage unless they are roasted with cheese or boiled to the point where they have lost most of their goodness.

This is where the NutriBullet comes in. It makes veggies taste great. A nutriblast can taste as good and as invigorating as a steak with fries or a cappuccino with a croissant or a chocolate torte with cream. Your mother would never have had to tell you to: "Eat your Greens" had your family possessed a NutriBullet.

The manufacturers claim all sorts of health benefits from it. And without going into medical detail, whatever the goodness is in a vegetable or leafy green or fruit or nut or seed, the NutriBullet can get that goodness out without destroying the delicate biochemical compounds with heat from cooking them. It is billed not as a blender or a juicer, but as an extractor. This is because the machine represents the best method mankind presently has of extracting the goodness from non meat food. The blades break down the cell walls of the ingredients and thereby release the cell contents into your intestines. So unless you have teeth which can rotate at 10,000 rpm, the NutriBullet represents a significant advance on chewing.

The other psychological trait of mankind which works against us here, is that we are loyal to what we like. Most of retail commerce is based upon brand loyalty. Although this type of loyalty doesn't always work so well with romantic partners! So we find a vegetable we like and then just eat that all the time. I mean once I have a record that I like, I will listen to it over and over again. So even if we do eat some vegetables or leafy greens or fruits, they will tend to be repetitions of a very small selection of what is available. They will just the ones that we have become familiar with and grown to like. They are essentially the vegetable next door.

So the purpose of this book is to empower to reader to vary their vegetables and fruits and greens and nuts and seeds on a daily basis. That is why we have included so many delicious Blasts and Smoothies. If you only drink a small fraction of these NutriBullet recipes you will be deficient in nothing that nature provides from Vegetables, Fruits, Nuts, Seeds and Greens.

Certain amino acids (protein) and fatty acids (fat) vitamins and minerals cannot be manufactured by the body. So they have to be eaten. This is one of the reasons why food variation is so important. Failing to eat certain essential foods can be lethal – even if you are putting on weight from all the food that you are eating! This was discovered when canned liquid diets were first invented. Some of the people who tried these out for more than a month just dropped dead due to running out of essential amino acids.

Essential Amino Acids

There are 11 of them: Tryptophan, Threonine, Isoleucine, Histidine Leucine, Lysine, Methionine + Cysteine, Phenylaneline + Tyrosine and Valine. These are nicely distributed throughout the leafy greens. Although meat and dairy have more protein and therefore more essential amino acids than greens per gram they have less protein than greens per kcal. So for dieters, Spinach (yummy) and Kale (fried or roasted in olive oil) are a good option.

Here are the Recommended Daily Intakes (RDI) or Recommended Daily Allowances (RDA) and Eastimated Average Requirements (EAR) for protein for 75kg/165lb men and for 64kg/140lb women.

Sex Age	EAR grams per day	RDI = RDA grams per day
165lb Men 19-30	52g	64g
165lb Men 30-50	52g	64g
165lb Men 50-70	52g	64g
165lb Men 70+	65g	81g
140lb Women 19-30	38g	48g
140lb Women 30-50	38g	48g
140lb Women 50-70	38g	48g
140lb Women 70+	48g	60g
140lb Pregnant Women	51g	64g
140lb Lactating Women	56g	70g

EAR is the estimated average requirement for 50% of people (i.e. for the average person) RDI/RDA is 20% higher and would work for 97% of the people. The figures are all linear so if you weight more then you should eat propoertionately more protein. RDI/RDA is 20% more than EAR.

The Essential Amino Acids should be eaten according to the following pattern in milligrams of essential amino acid per gram of protein intake...

Essential Amino Acid	RDI in mg per gram of Protein
Histidine	18mg
Isoleucine	25mg
Leucine	55mg
Lysine	51mg
Methionine + Cysteine	25mg
Phenylalanine + Tyrosine	47mg
Threonine	27mg
Tryptophan	7mg
Valine	32mg

So for a 75kg 50 year old man, with an RDI=RDA of 64grams of protein per day the Essential Amino Acid EARs are...

Essential Amino Acid	RDI in gram per day for a 64g perday Protein RDI
Histidine	1.15g
Isoleucine	1.64g
Leucine	3.52g
Lysine	3.26g
Methionine + Cysteine	1.60g
Phenylalanine + Tyrosine	3.01g
Threonine	1.73g
Tryptophan	0.45g
Valine	2.05g

One 200 ml glass of whole milk has between 24-42% of the Recommended Daily

Intake of all of the 9 essential amino acid groups. We use 200 ml of whole milk in some of our Blast and Smoothie Recipes.

Protein powder (from milk) can be added to Smoothies to boost the protein content (Whey, Soy, Pea or Rice Protein powders are readily available). This may be necessary for men on a low calorie diet. Good whey protein power has around 76 grams of protein per 100 grams of the powder which provides around 378 kcal of energy.

Essential Amino Acid	Grams per 50 grams of Whey Protein Powder
Histidine	0.65g
Isoleucine	2.35g
Leucine	3.95g
Lysine	3.55g
Methionine + Cysteine	1.60g
Phenylalanine + Tyrosine	2.05g
Threonine	2.5g
Tryptophan	0.50g
Valine	2.20g

50 grams of Whey Protein Powder, although having only 38 grams of protein within it will provide the full RDI of all essential amino acids for a 50 year old 75kg man except in the cases of Phenylalanine+Tyrosine where it only provides 68% (2.05g) of the RDI (3.01g) and Histidine where it only provides 56% (0.65g) of the RDI (1.15g).

This is why body builders use whey protein shakes. But low calorie dieters can benefit from them too. Women can just add 20 grams of whey protein powder and men can add 30 grams to a Nutribullet recipe and half of your essential amino acid requirements are met instantly.

Essential Vitamins

These are: A, B1 (Thiamin), B2 (Riboflavin), B3 (Niacin), B4 (Choline/Adenine)) B5 (Pantotheic Acid), B6 (Pyridoxines), B7 (Biotin)B9 (Folates), B12 (Cobalamin), C, D3, E, K

Stop Press: The latest EU guidelines for Vitamin D3 are now 4000 IU per day rather than 400! Also the latest research shows that high dose Vitamin D3 toxicity is caused by a lack of Vitamin K2. Spinach and Kale are rich in K1 which the body can convert into K2. But 100 micrograms of K2 supplementation (MK7 variety) is recommended for each 1000 IU of Vitamin D3. Vitamin K2 is expensive so eat your dark leafy greens!

Essential Oils and Fats

This is a very short list. Basically the more fish based Omega3 (EPA DHA in particular) the better up to around 5 grams per day. And the more seed nut or vegetable based Omega3 (ALA) the better without limit.

There is plenty of evidence that Omega 3 in your diet has a large effect upon the cardio vascular system. In particular the Omega3 fish based or vegetable and seed based fatty acids should be eaten in larger amounts if you are on a high fat diet. There are good Omega3 supplements out there but whole foods containing Omega3 normally provide better absorption into the body than Omega3 supplements.

The 10 Essential Minerals

Calcium, Copper, Iron, Magnesium, Manganese, Phosphours, Potassium, Selenium, Sodium, Zinc

25 Widely Recognized SuperFoods

These Superfoods contain many of the essential amino acids, fats, vitamins and minerals. But that is not why they are superfoods. They are defined as superfoods due to the health benefits that they confer. They are generally rich in anthocyanins, polyphenols, flavenoids, antioxidants, cancer fighting ellagic acid, heart disease fighting lycopene and other really useful nutrients which whilst not essential (in the sense that they can be manufactured by the body if it has the right components to hand), promote good health, fitness and well being. Between them these Superfoods are attributed with the following health benefits...

Increased Protection from Bacterial and Viral Infections
Increased Immune Function
Reduced Cancer Risk
Protection Against Heart Disease
Slowing Aging
DNA Repair and Protection
Prevention and reduction of Cardiovascular Disease
Reduced Hypertension (High Blood Pressure)
Alzheimer's Protection
Osteoporosis Protection
Stroke Prevention
Reduced Risk of Colon Cancer
Protection Against Heart Disease
Antioxidant Protection
Prevention of Epileptic Seizures
Prevention of Alopecia (Spot Baldness)

Reduced Risk of Type II Diabetes
Reduced Frequency of Migraine Headaches
Alleviation of Premenstrual Syndrome (PMS)
Regulation of Blood Sugar and Insulin Dependence
Slowing the progression of AIDS
Protection Against Dementia
Improved Eye Health
Alleviation of Inflammation
Alleviation of the Common Cold
Improving Sleep depth and length
Detoxing and Cleasning the body
Improving Bones Teeth Nerves and Muscle

Buckwheat and **Quinoa**: Too high in carbs to be included in our list and not suitable for a Blender Recipe

Chili Peppers and Garlic: Great but not really suitable for a Blender Recipe

Almonds: High in Protein, unsaturated Fat, Vitamins B1, B2, B3, B9, E, Calcium, Copper, Iron, Magnesium Phosphorus, Potassium, Zinc and Fibre

Dark Cholcolate: High in Protein, Saturated Fat, Vitamins B1, B2, B3, B9, K, Calcium, Copper, Magnesium Manganese, Phosphorus, Potassium, Selenium, Zinc and Fibre

Flax Seeds: High in Protein, unsaturated Fat, Vitamins B1, B3, B5, B6, B9, Calcium, Copper, Iron, Magnesium, Manganese, Phosphorus, Potassium, Selenium, Zinc, Fibre

Pumpkin Seeds: High in Protein,unsaturated Fat, Vitamins B2, B3, B5, B6, B9, E, Calcium, Copper, Iron, Magnesium, Manganese, Phosphorus, Potassium, Selenium, Zinc

Chia Seeds: High in Protein, has all essential amino acids in good quantity, incredibly high in Fibre at 34%, High in Omega3 at 17%, Vitamins B1, B2, B3, B9, Calcium, Copper Manganese, Phosphorus, Selenium, Zinc

Apricots: High in Vitamins A.C, E, Iron, Potassium, Fibre

Avocados: High in unsaturated Fat, Vitamins B2, B3, B5, B6, B9, C, K Cooper, Magnesium, Manganese and Potassium, Fibre

Blueberries: High in Vitamins B9, C, K, Manganese and Fibre

Raspberries: High in Vitamins B1, B2, B3, B9, C, K, Copper, Iron, Manganese and Fibre

Blackberries: High in Vitamins B9, C, K, Manganese and Fibre

Guavas: High in Vitamins: A, B9, C, Copper, Magnesium, Manganese, Potassium, Fibre

Papaya: High in Vitamins A, B9, C, Potassium, Fiber

Goji Berries: Contains all 11 Essential amino Acids - High in Vitamins A B2 C, Calcium, Selenium, Zinc, Iron, Potassium. But 46% Sugars. So not too many of them. Cures everything from impotence to malaria according to internet hype. Waitrose do them in the UK. Also called Wolfberries

Ginger: High in Vitamins B1, B2, B5, B6, C, Calcium, Copper, Iron, Magnesium, Manganese, Potassium, Selenium, Zinc, Fibre

Broccoli: High in Vitamins A, B1, B2, B5, B6, B9, C, K, Calcium, Iron, Magnesium, Manganese, Potassium

Carrots: High in Vitamins A, B3, B6, B9, C, K, Manganese, Potassium, Fibre

Tomatoes: High in Vitamins A, B2, B6, B9 C, Potassium, Lycopene

Beetroot: Vitamin B6, B9, C, Iron, Magnesium, Manganese, Phosphorus, Potassium, Zinc, Fibre

Kale: High in Vitamins A, B1, B2, B3, B6, B9, C, K, Calcium, Copper, Iron, Magnesium, Manganese, Potassium

Spinach: High in Vitamins A, B2, B6, B9, C, E, K, Calcium, Copper, Iron. Magnesium, Manganese, Potassium, Fibre

Swiss Chard: High in Vitamins A, C, E, K, Calcium, Copper, Iron, Magensium, Manganese, Potassium, Sodium

Hence we include many Superfood Blast and Smoothie Recipes!

Eat a Rainbow of Colour

Red - Lyopene, anthocyanins and other phytonutrients found in red fruits and veggies. Lycopene is a powerful antioxidant that can help reduce the risk of cancer and keep our heart healthy and improve memory function.

White/Tan - Contrary to popular belief, white foods aren't so useless after all! These foods have been shown to reduce the risk of certain cancers, balance hormone levels, lower blood pressure, and boost your body's natural immunity with nutrients such as EGCG and allicin. White fruits and vegetables contain a range of health-promoting phytochemicals such as allicin (found in garlic) which is known for its antiviral and antibacterial properties. Some members of the white group, such as bananas and potatoes, are also a good source of potassium.

Green - Chlorophyll-rich detoxification properties are the most noted value in leafy greens. In addition, luteins, zeaxanthin, along with indoles, help boost greens' cancer-fighting properties, encourage vision health, and help build strong bones and teeth. Green vegetables contain a range of phytochemicals including carotenoids, indoles and saponins, all of which have anti-cancer properties. Leafy greens such as spinach and broccoli are also excellent sources of folate.

Blue/Purple - Phytochemicals anthocyanin and resveratrol promote youthful skin, hair and nails. In addition, these anti-inflammatory compounds may also play a role in cancer-prevention, especially skin cancer and urinary and digestive tract health. They may also reduce the risk of cardio vascular disease.

Orange/Yellow - Foods glowing with orange and yellow are great immune-boosters and vision protectors, mainly due to their high levels of carotenoids. Carotenoids give this group their vibrant colour. A well-known carotenoid called Betacarotene is found in sweet potatoes, pumpkins and carrots. It is converted to vitamin A, which helps maintain healthy mucous membranes and healthy eyes. Another carotenoid called lutein is stored in the eye and has been found to prevent cataracts and age-related macular degeneration, which can lead to blindness.

(Information from Nutrition Australia and NutriBullet Blog)

Nutrition Data

All our Blasts and Smoothies come with full nutritional data giving the precise number of grams of Protein, Carbohydrate, Fat and Fibre for each recipe and the number of Kcals it contains. The data is taken mainly from the USDA. database.

NutriBullet Capacities

US traditional cup is 8 US fluid oz or 240 ml (236 ml to be exact). However putting berries or slices or cubes of fruit and veggies into a cup wastes around 50% of the space so in weight terms an 8 fluid oz cup will contain around 4 oz or 120 grams of contents.

Greens use even less of the space, so 2 Cups/Handfuls of Spinach or Kale will only weigh around 40/50 grams.

There are 28 grams in a British Imperial fluid ounce, which is 4% larger than the US fluid ounce - which is pretty unhelpful. So it is easier just to take 28 grams for an ounce in both cases.

The NutriBullet tall cup takes 590 ml/grams of water up to the MAX fill line. The small cup takes 305 grams of water up to the MAX fill line.

All our recipes are designed and stated for the standard tall cup (28 oz total, 24 oz to max fill).

To use the small cup you just halve them all!

The entire tall cup can take around 826 ml/grams of water up to the top. This is 3½ standard US cups or 28 fluid ounces. However we can put 4¼ cups worth of greens, veggies, fruits, nuts and seeds into the tall cup because they compress a lot when they lose their shape after blasting.

All ingredients are stated in Cups and Handfuls or Grams and American Ounces (oz)

CLEANING

Cleaning

The NutriBullet is easy to clean. The manufacturers recommend warm water (not hot) and a mild detergent. Rinse the blades and the cups and the base (if necessary) immediately after use to prevent the debris from drying.

Warnings

Do not put your hand or any implement near the blades when the NutriBullet is plugged in to an electricity supply.

Flat Leaf Kale not Curly Kale

Kale is a Superfood and is very good for you. But Curly Kale does not taste as good as the other greens in a NutriBlast in our opinion! To be frank, it tastes like cardboard. However flat leaf Kale, with the leaves pulled off the stems taste wonderful and is not too fibrous. So we have specified flat leaf de-stemmed Kale in our recipes.

AVOID THESE INGREDIENTS: Apple Pear Peach Plum Apricot and Cherry **stones and pips** contain cyanide which is very poisonous. These stones and pips *must* therefore be removed before use!

Rhubarb leaves contain oxalate which causes kidney stones, comas, convulsions. 5lb of Rhubarb leaves is fatal!

Tomatoes are fine but the **tomato leaves and vines** are not. They contain alkaloid poisons such as atropine which causes headaches dizziness and vomiting.

Nutmeg: Contains myristicine which is halucingoenic and causes dizziness and vomiting. It is OK in small quantities as a spice but we do not recommend it for the NutriBullet.

Kidney Beans and **Lima Beans**: These are really really poisonous if eaten raw.

TIPS & EXTRAS

Tips and Extras

Cinnamon and Cloves are lovely in a hot drink but do not really work in a cold one such as a Nutribullet blast. We cannot recommend adding sugar given the health difficulties associated with refined sucrose. But the following are fantastic in Nutriblasts...

Ginger Root (sliced)
Lemon Juice
Lime Juice
Agave Nectar
Honey
Garlic Cloves
Cocoa Powder which is also called Cacao Powder (a Superfood)
85% Dark Chocolate (a Superfood)
Maca Powder (a Superfood)
Instant Coffee
Coriander
Basil
Parsley
Sage
Chives
Chlorella Powder (Detoxing supergreen 50% protein algae)
Spirulina Powder
(Supergreen immunity boosting 57% protein algae)
Whey Protein Powder
(Banana, Chocolate, Cookies, Strawberry flavours etc.) – for extra protein
Rice Protein Powder
Pea Protein Powder
Soy Protein Powder

These can be added to any of the recipes for a taste or nutrition boost.

THE RECIPES

Mega Low Carb Smoothies
(With no more than 5 Carb Grams)

The Works

Ingredients

1¼ Cup/Handful of Swiss Chard (50 grams or 1¾ oz)
1¼ Cup/Handful of Broccoli florets (50 grams or 1¾ oz)
1¼ Cup/Handful of Spinach florets (50 grams or 1¾ oz)
1¼ Cup/Handful of de-stemmed Balck Kale (50 grams or 1¾ oz)
150 ml / 5 fl oz of Almond Milk (Unsweetened)

Protein 6.2g, Fat 3.38g, Carb 4.9g, Fibre 5.1g, 79 Kcals

Preparation

Place the nuts or seeds into the Tall Cup. Screw the Nutribullet Extractor Blade on to the top of the cup. Invert the cup, press it down into the Nutribullet Power Base and twist it into place. Blast them for 30 seconds. Put the rest of the solid ingredients into the cup and press them down below the Max Line. Add the fluid base to fill the cup up to the Max Line. Screw the Nutribullet Extractor Blade on to the top of the cup. Invert the cup, press it down into the Nutribullet Power Base and twist it into place. Blast the mixture until it is really smooth (20 or so seconds). **Enjoy!**

Spinach and Kale 4 Health

Ingredients

2½ Cups/Handfuls of Spinach (100 grams or 3½ oz)
2½ Cups/Handfuls of Black Kale (destemmed) (100 grams or 3½ oz)
½ Cup/Handful of sliced fine beans (40 grams or 1½ oz)
150 ml / 5 fl oz of Almond Milk (Unsweetened)

Protein 7.6g, Fat 3.8g, Carb 4.7g, Fibre 6g, 88 Kcals

Preparation

Place the nuts or seeds into the Tall Cup. Screw the Nutribullet Extractor Blade on to the top of the cup. Invert the cup, press it down into the Nutribullet Power Base and twist it into place. Blast them for 30 seconds. Put the rest of the solid ingredients into the cup and press them down below the Max Line. Add the fluid base to fill the cup up to the Max Line. Screw the Nutribullet Extractor Blade on to the top of the cup. Invert the cup, press it down into the Nutribullet Power Base and twist it into place. Blast the mixture until it is really smooth (20 or so seconds). **Enjoy!**

Strawberry Surprise

Ingredients

2 Cups/Handfuls of Swiss Chard (80 grams or 3 oz)
2½ Cups/Handfuls of Spinach (100 grams or 3½ oz)
½ Cup/Handful of sliced Strawberry (30 grams or 1 oz)
150 ml / 5 fl oz of Almond Milk (Unsweetened)

Protein 5.1g, Fat 2.3g, Carb 5.0g, Fibre 4.7g, 67 Kcals

Preparation

Place the nuts or seeds into the Tall Cup. Screw the Nutribullet Extractor Blade on to the top of the cup. Invert the cup, press it down into the Nutribullet Power Base and twist it into place. Blast them for 30 seconds. Put the rest of the solid ingredients into the cup and press them down below the Max Line. Add the fluid base to fill the cup up to the Max Line. Screw the Nutribullet Extractor Blade on to the top of the cup. Invert the cup, press it down into the Nutribullet Power Base and twist it into place. Blast the mixture until it is really smooth (20 or so seconds). **Enjoy!**

Ultra Low Carb Superfood Blasts
Made entirely out of Superfoods and Cucumber

Chard Cornucopia

Ingredients

1 Cup/Handful of Swiss Chard (40 grams or 1½ oz)
1 Cup/Handful of Spinach (40 grams or 1½ oz)
½ Cup of Avocado slices (60 grams or 2 oz)
1 Cup/Handful of sliced Asparagus (120 grams or 4 oz)
22 grams or ¾ oz of Chia Seeds
150 ml / 5 fl oz of Almond Milk (Unsweetened)

Protein 10g, Fat 18g, Carb 7g, Fibre 16g, 263 Kcals

Preparation

Place the nuts or seeds into the Tall Cup. Screw the Nutribullet Extractor Blade on to the top of the cup. Invert the cup, press it down into the Nutribullet Power Base and twist it into place. Blast them for 30 seconds. Put the rest of the solid ingredients into the cup and press them down below the Max Line. Add the fluid base to fill the cup up to the Max Line. Screw the Nutribullet Extractor Blade on to the top of the cup. Invert the cup, press it down into the Nutribullet Power Base and twist it into place. Blast the mixture until it is really smooth (20 or so seconds). **Enjoy!**

Chard and Avocado Dictator

Ingredients

1 Cup/Handful of Swiss Chard (40 grams or 1½ oz)
1 Cup/Handful of Broccoli Florets (40 grams or 1½ oz)
½ Cup of Avocado slices (60 grams or 2 oz)
1 Cup/Handful of sliced Tomato (120 grams or 4 oz)
22 grams or ¾ oz of Flax Seeds
150 ml / 5 fl oz of Almond Milk (Unsweetened)

Protein 9g, Fat 20g, Carb 7g, Fibre 14g, 275 Kcals

Preparation

Place the nuts or seeds into the Tall Cup. Screw the Nutribullet Extractor Blade on to the top of the cup. Invert the cup, press it down into the Nutribullet Power Base and twist it into place. Blast them for 30 seconds. Put the rest of the solid ingredients into the cup and press them down below the Max Line. Add the fluid base to fill the cup up to the Max Line. Screw the Nutribullet Extractor Blade on to the top of the cup. Invert the cup, press it down into the Nutribullet Power Base and twist it into place. Blast the mixture until it is really smooth (20 or so seconds). **Enjoy!**

Broccoli in Avocado

Ingredients

1 Cup/Handful of Spinach (40 grams or 1½ oz)
1 Cup/Handful of Broccoli Florets (40 grams or 1½ oz)
½ Cup of Avocado slices (60 grams or 2 oz)
1 Cup/Handful of sliced Asparagus (120 grams or 4 oz)
22 grams or ¾ oz of Chia Seeds
150 ml / 5 fl oz of Almond Milk (Unsweetened)

Protein 10g, Fat 18g, Carb 7g, Fibre 17g, 269 Kcals

Preparation

Place the nuts or seeds into the Tall Cup. Screw the Nutribullet Extractor Blade on to the top of the cup. Invert the cup, press it down into the Nutribullet Power Base and twist it into place. Blast them for 30 seconds. Put the rest of the solid ingredients into the cup and press them down below the Max Line. Add the fluid base to fill the cup up to the Max Line. Screw the Nutribullet Extractor Blade on to the top of the cup. Invert the cup, press it down into the Nutribullet Power Base and twist it into place. Blast the mixture until it is really smooth (20 or so seconds). **Enjoy!**

Chard and Raspberry Splash

Ingredients

2 Cups/Handfuls of Swiss Chard (80 grams or 3 oz)
½ Cup of Raspberries (60 grams or 2 oz)
1 Cup/Handful of sliced Asparagus (120 grams or 4 oz)
22 grams or ¾ oz of Flax Seeds
150 ml / 5 fl oz of Almond Milk (Unsweetened)

Protein 9g, Fat 12g, Carb 8g, Fibre 14g, 207 Kcals

Preparation

Place the nuts or seeds into the Tall Cup. Screw the Nutribullet Extractor Blade on to the top of the cup. Invert the cup, press it down into the Nutribullet Power Base and twist it into place. Blast them for 30 seconds. Put the rest of the solid ingredients into the cup and press them down below the Max Line. Add the fluid base to fill the cup up to the Max Line. Screw the Nutribullet Extractor Blade on to the top of the cup. Invert the cup, press it down into the Nutribullet Power Base and twist it into place. Blast the mixture until it is really smooth (20 or so seconds). **Enjoy!**

Black Kale Blizzard

Ingredients

1 Cup/Handful of Swiss Chard (40 grams or 1½ oz)
1 Cup/Handful of Black Kale de-stemmed (40 grams or 1½ oz)
½ Cup of Avocado slices (60 grams or 2 oz)
1 Cup/Handful of sliced Tomato (120 grams or 4 oz)
22 grams or ¾ oz of Chia Seeds
150 ml / 5 fl oz of Almond Milk (Unsweetened)

Protein 9g, Fat 18g, Carb 8g, Fibre 15g, 265 Kcals

Preparation

Place the nuts or seeds into the Tall Cup. Screw the Nutribullet Extractor Blade on to the top of the cup. Invert the cup, press it down into the Nutribullet Power Base and twist it into place. Blast them for 30 seconds. Put the rest of the solid ingredients into the cup and press them down below the Max Line. Add the fluid base to fill the cup up to the Max Line. Screw the Nutribullet Extractor Blade on to the top of the cup. Invert the cup, press it down into the Nutribullet Power Base and twist it into place. Blast the mixture until it is really smooth (20 or so seconds). **Enjoy!**

Spinach Sonata

Ingredients

1 Cup/Handful of Spinach (40 grams or 1½ oz)
1 Cup/Handful of Black Kale de-stemmed (40 grams or 1½ oz)
½ Cup of Blackberries (60 grams or 2 oz)
1 Cup/Handful of sliced Asparagus (120 grams or 4 oz)
22 grams or ¾ oz of Chia Seeds
150 ml / 5 fl oz of Almond Milk (Unsweetened)

Protein 10g, Fat 10g, Carb 8g, Fibre 16g, 199 Kcals

Preparation

Place the nuts or seeds into the Tall Cup. Screw the Nutribullet Extractor Blade on to the top of the cup. Invert the cup, press it down into the Nutribullet Power Base and twist it into place. Blast them for 30 seconds. Put the rest of the solid ingredients into the cup and press them down below the Max Line. Add the fluid base to fill the cup up to the Max Line. Screw the Nutribullet Extractor Blade on to the top of the cup. Invert the cup, press it down into the Nutribullet Power Base and twist it into place. Blast the mixture until it is really smooth (20 or so seconds). ***Enjoy!***

Tomato Tango

Ingredients

2 Cups/Handfuls of Swiss Chard (80 grams or 3 oz)
½ Cup of Avocado slices (60 grams or 2 oz)
1 Cup/Handful of sliced Tomato (120 grams or 4 oz)
22 grams or ¾ oz of Pumpkin Seeds
150 ml / 5 fl oz of Almond Milk (Unsweetened)

Protein 10g, Fat 21g, Carb 8g, Fibre 9g, 276 Kcals

Preparation

Place the nuts or seeds into the Tall Cup. Screw the Nutribullet Extractor Blade on to the top of the cup. Invert the cup, press it down into the Nutribullet Power Base and twist it into place. Blast them for 30 seconds. Put the rest of the solid ingredients into the cup and press them down below the Max Line. Add the fluid base to fill the cup up to the Max Line. Screw the Nutribullet Extractor Blade on to the top of the cup. Invert the cup, press it down into the Nutribullet Power Base and twist it into place. Blast the mixture until it is really smooth (20 or so seconds). ***Enjoy!***

Spinach needs Chia

Ingredients

1 Cup/Handful of Broccoli Florets (40 grams or 1½ oz)
1 Cup/Handful of Spinach (40 grams or 1½ oz)
½ Cup of Avocado slices (60 grams or 2 oz)
1 Cup/Handful of sliced Tomato (120 grams or 4 oz)
22 grams or ¾ oz of Chia Seeds
150 ml / 5 fl oz of Almond Milk (Unsweetened)

Protein 9g, Fat 18g, Carb 8g, Fibre 16g, 266 Kcals

Preparation

Place the nuts or seeds into the Tall Cup. Screw the Nutribullet Extractor Blade on to the top of the cup. Invert the cup, press it down into the Nutribullet Power Base and twist it into place. Blast them for 30 seconds. Put the rest of the solid ingredients into the cup and press them down below the Max Line. Add the fluid base to fill the cup up to the Max Line. Screw the Nutribullet Extractor Blade on to the top of the cup. Invert the cup, press it down into the Nutribullet Power Base and twist it into place. Blast the mixture until it is really smooth (20 or so seconds). **Enjoy!**

Raspberry in Flax

Ingredients

1 Cup/Handful of Black Kale de-stemmed (40 grams or 1½ oz)
1 Cup/Handful of Swiss Chard (40 grams or 1½ oz)
½ Cup of Raspberries (60 grams or 2 oz)
1 Cup/Handful of sliced Tomato (120 grams or 4 oz)
22 grams or ¾ oz of Flax Seeds
150 ml / 5 fl oz of Almond Milk (Unsweetened)

Protein 8g, Fat 12g, Carb 9g, Fibre 14g, 211 Kcals

Preparation

Place the nuts or seeds into the Tall Cup. Screw the Nutribullet Extractor Blade on to the top of the cup. Invert the cup, press it down into the Nutribullet Power Base and twist it into place. Blast them for 30 seconds. Put the rest of the solid ingredients into the cup and press them down below the Max Line. Add the fluid base to fill the cup up to the Max Line. Screw the Nutribullet Extractor Blade on to the top of the cup. Invert the cup, press it down into the Nutribullet Power Base and twist it into place. Blast the mixture until it is really smooth (20 or so seconds). **Enjoy!**

Spinach and Pumpkin Creation

Ingredients

1 Cup/Handful of Spinach (40 grams or 1½ oz)
1 Cup/Handful of Broccoli Florets (40 grams or 1½ oz)
½ Cup of Blackberries (60 grams or 2 oz)
1 Cup/Handful of sliced Asparagus (120 grams or 4 oz)
22 grams or ¾ oz of Pumpkin Seeds
150 ml / 5 fl oz of Almond Milk (Unsweetened)

Protein 12g, Fat 12g, Carb 9g, Fibre 9g, 216 Kcals

Preparation

Place the nuts or seeds into the Tall Cup. Screw the Nutribullet Extractor Blade on to the top of the cup. Invert the cup, press it down into the Nutribullet Power Base and twist it into place. Blast them for 30 seconds. Put the rest of the solid ingredients into the cup and press them down below the Max Line. Add the fluid base to fill the cup up to the Max Line. Screw the Nutribullet Extractor Blade on to the top of the cup. Invert the cup, press it down into the Nutribullet Power Base and twist it into place. Blast the mixture until it is really smooth (20 or so seconds). *Enjoy!*

Pumpkin Perfection

Ingredients

1 Cup/Handful of Spinach (40 grams or 1½ oz)
1 Cup/Handful of Black Kale de-stemmed (40 grams or 1½ oz)
½ Cup of Blackberries (60 grams or 2 oz)
1 Cup/Handful of sliced Tomato (120 grams or 4 oz)
22 grams or ¾ oz of Pumpkin Seeds
150 ml / 5 fl oz of Almond Milk (Unsweetened)

Protein 10g, Fat 13g, Carb 9g, Fibre 8g, 214 Kcals

Preparation

Place the nuts or seeds into the Tall Cup. Screw the Nutribullet Extractor Blade on to the top of the cup. Invert the cup, press it down into the Nutribullet Power Base and twist it into place. Blast them for 30 seconds. Put the rest of the solid ingredients into the cup and press them down below the Max Line. Add the fluid base to fill the cup up to the Max Line. Screw the Nutribullet Extractor Blade on to the top of the cup. Invert the cup, press it down into the Nutribullet Power Base and twist it into place. Blast the mixture until it is really smooth (20 or so seconds). *Enjoy!*

Asparagus Amazement

Ingredients

2 Cups/Handfuls of Black Kale de-stemmed (80 grams or 3 oz)
½ Cup of Papaya (60 grams or 2 oz)
1 Cup/Handful of sliced Asparagus (120 grams or 4 oz)
22 grams or ¾ oz of Flax Seeds
150 ml / 5 fl oz of Almond Milk (Unsweetened)

Protein 10g, Fat 13g, Carb 10g, Fibre 12g, 214 Kcals

Preparation

Place the nuts or seeds into the Tall Cup. Screw the Nutribullet Extractor Blade on to the top of the cup. Invert the cup, press it down into the Nutribullet Power Base and twist it into place. Blast them for 30 seconds. Put the rest of the solid ingredients into the cup and press them down below the Max Line. Add the fluid base to fill the cup up to the Max Line. Screw the Nutribullet Extractor Blade on to the top of the cup. Invert the cup, press it down into the Nutribullet Power Base and twist it into place. Blast the mixture until it is really smooth (20 or so seconds). **Enjoy!**

Chard and Flax Waterfall

Ingredients

2 Cups/Handfuls of Swiss Chard (80 grams or 3 oz)
½ Cup of Apricot halves (60 grams or 2 oz)
1 Cup/Handful of sliced Asparagus (120 grams or 4 oz)
22 grams or ¾ oz of Flax Seeds
150 ml / 5 fl oz of Almond Milk (Unsweetened)

Protein 10g, Fat 11g, Carb 10g, Fibre 11g, 204 Kcals

Preparation

Place the nuts or seeds into the Tall Cup. Screw the Nutribullet Extractor Blade on to the top of the cup. Invert the cup, press it down into the Nutribullet Power Base and twist it into place. Blast them for 30 seconds. Put the rest of the solid ingredients into the cup and press them down below the Max Line. Add the fluid base to fill the cup up to the Max Line. Screw the Nutribullet Extractor Blade on to the top of the cup. Invert the cup, press it down into the Nutribullet Power Base and twist it into place. Blast the mixture until it is really smooth (20 or so seconds). **Enjoy!**

Broccoli Breeze

Ingredients

1 Cup/Handful of Broccoli Florets (40 grams or 1½ oz)
1 Cup/Handful of Swiss Chard (40 grams or 1½ oz)
½ Cup of Raspberries (60 grams or 2 oz)
1 Cup/Handful of sliced Asparagus (120 grams or 4 oz)
22 grams or ¾ oz of Pumpkin Seeds
150 ml / 5 fl oz of Almond Milk (Unsweetened)

Protein 11g, Fat 12g, Carb 10g, Fibre 10g, 220 Kcals

Preparation

Place the nuts or seeds into the Tall Cup. Screw the Nutribullet Extractor Blade on to the top of the cup. Invert the cup, press it down into the Nutribullet Power Base and twist it into place. Blast them for 30 seconds. Put the rest of the solid ingredients into the cup and press them down below the Max Line. Add the fluid base to fill the cup up to the Max Line. Screw the Nutribullet Extractor Blade on to the top of the cup. Invert the cup, press it down into the Nutribullet Power Base and twist it into place. Blast the mixture until it is really smooth (20 or so seconds). **Enjoy!**

Broccoli and Blackberry Kiss

Ingredients

2 Cups/Handfuls of Broccoli Florets (80 grams or 3 oz)
½ Cup of Blackberries (60 grams or 2 oz)
1 Cup/Handful of sliced Asparagus (120 grams or 4 oz)
30 grams or 1 oz of Almonds
150 ml / 5 fl oz of Almond Milk (Unsweetened)

Protein 13g, Fat 18g, Carb 10g, Fibre 11g, 273 Kcals

Preparation

Place the nuts or seeds into the Tall Cup. Screw the Nutribullet Extractor Blade on to the top of the cup. Invert the cup, press it down into the Nutribullet Power Base and twist it into place. Blast them for 30 seconds. Put the rest of the solid ingredients into the cup and press them down below the Max Line. Add the fluid base to fill the cup up to the Max Line. Screw the Nutribullet Extractor Blade on to the top of the cup. Invert the cup, press it down into the Nutribullet Power Base and twist it into place. Blast the mixture until it is really smooth (20 or so seconds). **Enjoy!**

Almond Avarice

Ingredients

2 Cups/Handfuls of Swiss Chard (80 grams or 3 oz)
½ Cup of Raspberries (60 grams or 2 oz)
1 Cup/Handful of sliced Tomato (120 grams or 4 oz)
30 grams or 1 oz of Almonds
150 ml / 5 fl oz of Almond Milk (Unsweetened)

Protein 10g, Fat 18g, Carb 10g, Fibre 10g, 264 Kcals

Preparation

Place the nuts or seeds into the Tall Cup. Screw the Nutribullet Extractor Blade on to the top of the cup. Invert the cup, press it down into the Nutribullet Power Base and twist it into place. Blast them for 30 seconds. Put the rest of the solid ingredients into the cup and press them down below the Max Line. Add the fluid base to fill the cup up to the Max Line. Screw the Nutribullet Extractor Blade on to the top of the cup. Invert the cup, press it down into the Nutribullet Power Base and twist it into place. Blast the mixture until it is really smooth (20 or so seconds). **Enjoy!**

Black Kale on Blackberry

Ingredients

1 Cup/Handful of Black Kale de-stemmed (40 grams or 1½ oz)
1 Cup/Handful of Broccoli Florets (40 grams or 1½ oz)
½ Cup of Blackberries (60 grams or 2 oz)
1 Cup/Handful of sliced Tomato (120 grams or 4 oz)
22 grams or ¾ oz of Pumpkin Seeds
150 ml / 5 fl oz of Almond Milk (Unsweetened)

Protein 10g, Fat 13g, Carb 10g, Fibre 8g, 218 Kcals

Preparation

Place the nuts or seeds into the Tall Cup. Screw the Nutribullet Extractor Blade on to the top of the cup. Invert the cup, press it down into the Nutribullet Power Base and twist it into place. Blast them for 30 seconds. Put the rest of the solid ingredients into the cup and press them down below the Max Line. Add the fluid base to fill the cup up to the Max Line. Screw the Nutribullet Extractor Blade on to the top of the cup. Invert the cup, press it down into the Nutribullet Power Base and twist it into place. Blast the mixture until it is really smooth (20 or so seconds). **Enjoy!**

Papaya Panacea

Ingredients

2 Cups/Handfuls of Black Kale de-stemmed (80 grams or 3 oz)
½ Cup of Papaya (60 grams or 2 oz)
1 Cup/Handful of sliced Tomato (120 grams or 4 oz)
22 grams or ¾ oz of Flax Seeds
150 ml / 5 fl oz of Almond Milk (Unsweetened)

Protein 9g, Fat 13g, Carb 11g, Fibre 11g, 212 Kcals

Preparation

Place the nuts or seeds into the Tall Cup. Screw the Nutribullet Extractor Blade on to the top of the cup. Invert the cup, press it down into the Nutribullet Power Base and twist it into place. Blast them for 30 seconds. Put the rest of the solid ingredients into the cup and press them down below the Max Line. Add the fluid base to fill the cup up to the Max Line. Screw the Nutribullet Extractor Blade on to the top of the cup. Invert the cup, press it down into the Nutribullet Power Base and twist it into place. Blast the mixture until it is really smooth (20 or so seconds). **Enjoy!**

Broccoli and Chia Blossom

Ingredients

1 Cup/Handful of Swiss Chard (40 grams or 1½ oz)
1 Cup/Handful of Broccoli Florets (40 grams or 1½ oz)
½ Cup of Raspberries (60 grams or 2 oz)
1 Cup/Handful of sliced Tomato (120 grams or 4 oz)
22 grams or ¾ oz of Chia Seeds
150 ml / 5 fl oz of Almond Milk (Unsweetened)

Protein 8g, Fat 9g, Carb 11g, Fibre 15g, 200 Kcals

Preparation

Place the nuts or seeds into the Tall Cup. Screw the Nutribullet Extractor Blade on to the top of the cup. Invert the cup, press it down into the Nutribullet Power Base and twist it into place. Blast them for 30 seconds. Put the rest of the solid ingredients into the cup and press them down below the Max Line. Add the fluid base to fill the cup up to the Max Line. Screw the Nutribullet Extractor Blade on to the top of the cup. Invert the cup, press it down into the Nutribullet Power Base and twist it into place. Blast the mixture until it is really smooth (20 or so seconds). **Enjoy!**

Chard and Papaya Treat

Ingredients

1 Cup/Handful of Swiss Chard (40 grams or 1½ oz)
1 Cup/Handful of Spinach (40 grams or 1½ oz)
½ Cup of Papaya (60 grams or 2 oz)
1 Cup/Handful of sliced Asparagus (120 grams or 4 oz)
22 grams or ¾ oz of Chia Seeds
150 ml / 5 fl oz of Almond Milk (Unsweetened)

Protein 9g, Fat 9g, Carb 11g, Fibre 13g, 193 Kcals

Preparation

Place the nuts or seeds into the Tall Cup. Screw the Nutribullet Extractor Blade on to the top of the cup. Invert the cup, press it down into the Nutribullet Power Base and twist it into place. Blast them for 30 seconds. Put the rest of the solid ingredients into the cup and press them down below the Max Line. Add the fluid base to fill the cup up to the Max Line. Screw the Nutribullet Extractor Blade on to the top of the cup. Invert the cup, press it down into the Nutribullet Power Base and twist it into place. Blast the mixture until it is really smooth (20 or so seconds). **Enjoy!**

Ultra Low Carb Superfood Smoothies
Made entirely out of Superfoods and Cucumber

Spinach on Black Kale

Ingredients

1 Cup/Handful of Spinach (40 grams or 1½ oz)
1 Cup/Handful of Black Kale de-stemmed (40 grams or 1½ oz)
½ Cup of Avocado slices (60 grams or 2 oz)
1 Cup/Handful of sliced Asparagus (120 grams or 4 oz)
150 ml / 5 fl oz of Almond Milk (Unsweetened)

Protein 7g, Fat 11g, Carb 5g, Fibre 9g, 162 Kcals

Preparation

Put all the solid ingredients into the Tall Cup and press them down below the Max Line. Add the fluid base to fill the cup up to the Max Line. Screw the Nutribullet Extractor Blade on to the top of the cup. Invert the cup, press it down into the Nutribullet Power Base and twist it into place. Blast the mixture until it is really smooth (20 or so seconds). **Enjoy!**

Chard needs Spinach

Ingredients

1 Cup/Handful of Swiss Chard (40 grams or 1½ oz)
1 Cup/Handful of Spinach (40 grams or 1½ oz)
½ Cup of Avocado slices (60 grams or 2 oz)
1 Cup/Handful of sliced Asparagus (120 grams or 4 oz)
150 ml / 5 fl oz of Almond Milk (Unsweetened)

Protein 6g, Fat 11g, Carb 5g, Fibre 9g, 156 Kcals

Preparation

Put all the solid ingredients into the Tall Cup and press them down below the Max Line. Add the fluid base to fill the cup up to the Max Line. Screw the Nutribullet Extractor Blade on to the top of the cup. Invert the cup, press it down into the Nutribullet Power Base and twist it into place. Blast the mixture until it is really smooth (20 or so seconds). *Enjoy!*

Black Kale meets Chard

Ingredients

1 Cup/Handful of Black Kale de-stemmed (40 grams or 1½ oz)
1 Cup/Handful of Swiss Chard (40 grams or 1½ oz)
½ Cup of Avocado slices (60 grams or 2 oz)
1 Cup/Handful of sliced Asparagus (120 grams or 4 oz)
150 ml / 5 fl oz of Almond Milk (Unsweetened)

Protein 7g, Fat 11g, Carb 5g, Fibre 9g, 161 Kcals

Preparation

Put all the solid ingredients into the Tall Cup and press them down below the Max Line. Add the fluid base to fill the cup up to the Max Line. Screw the Nutribullet Extractor Blade on to the top of the cup. Invert the cup, press it down into the Nutribullet Power Base and twist it into place. Blast the mixture until it is really smooth (20 or so seconds). *Enjoy!*

Veggie Revelation

Ingredients

2 Cups/Handfuls of Swiss Chard (80 grams or 3 oz)
½ Cup of Avocado slices (60 grams or 2 oz)
1 Cup/Handful of sliced Asparagus (120 grams or 4 oz)
150 ml / 5 fl oz of Almond Milk (Unsweetened)

Protein 6g, Fat 11g, Carb 5g, Fibre 8g, 154 Kcals

Preparation

Put all the solid ingredients into the Tall Cup and press them down below the Max Line. Add the fluid base to fill the cup up to the Max Line. Screw the Nutribullet Extractor Blade on to the top of the cup. Invert the cup, press it down into the Nutribullet Power Base and twist it into place. Blast the mixture until it is really smooth (20 or so seconds). **Enjoy!**

Verdant Indulgence

Ingredients

2 Cups/Handfuls of Black Kale de-stemmed (80 grams or 3 oz)
½ Cup of Blackberries (60 grams or 2 oz)
1 Cup/Handful of sliced Asparagus (120 grams or 4 oz)
150 ml / 5 fl oz of Almond Milk (Unsweetened)

Protein 7g, Fat 3g, Carb 6g, Fibre 8g, 97 Kcals

Preparation

Put all the solid ingredients into the Tall Cup and press them down below the Max Line. Add the fluid base to fill the cup up to the Max Line. Screw the Nutribullet Extractor Blade on to the top of the cup. Invert the cup, press it down into the Nutribullet Power Base and twist it into place. Blast the mixture until it is really smooth (20 or so seconds). **Enjoy!**

Verdant Perfection

Ingredients

1 Cup/Handful of Broccoli Florets (40 grams or 1½ oz)
1 Cup/Handful of Swiss Chard (40 grams or 1½ oz)
½ Cup of Avocado slices (60 grams or 2 oz)
1 Cup/Handful of sliced Tomato (120 grams or 4 oz)
150 ml / 5 fl oz of Almond Milk (Unsweetened)

Protein 5g, Fat 11g, Carb 7g, Fibre 8g, 158 Kcals

Preparation

Put all the solid ingredients into the Tall Cup and press them down below the Max Line. Add the fluid base to fill the cup up to the Max Line. Screw the Nutribullet Extractor Blade on to the top of the cup. Invert the cup, press it down into the Nutribullet Power Base and twist it into place. Blast the mixture until it is really smooth (20 or so seconds). ***Enjoy!***

Raspberry in Asparagus

Ingredients

1 Cup/Handful of Swiss Chard (40 grams or 1½ oz)
1 Cup/Handful of Spinach (40 grams or 1½ oz)
½ Cup of Raspberries (60 grams or 2 oz)
1 Cup/Handful of sliced Asparagus (120 grams or 4 oz)
150 ml / 5 fl oz of Almond Milk (Unsweetened)

Protein 6g, Fat 2g, Carb 7g, Fibre 8g, 91 Kcals

Preparation

Put all the solid ingredients into the Tall Cup and press them down below the Max Line. Add the fluid base to fill the cup up to the Max Line. Screw the Nutribullet Extractor Blade on to the top of the cup. Invert the cup, press it down into the Nutribullet Power Base and twist it into place. Blast the mixture until it is really smooth (20 or so seconds). ***Enjoy!***

Green City

Ingredients

1 Cup/Handful of Spinach (40 grams or 1½ oz)
1 Cup/Handful of Black Kale de-stemmed (40 grams or 1½ oz)
½ Cup of Blackberries (60 grams or 2 oz)
1 Cup/Handful of sliced Tomato (120 grams or 4 oz)
150 ml / 5 fl oz of Almond Milk (Unsweetened)

Protein 5g, Fat 3g, Carb 7g, Fibre 7g, 90 Kcals

Preparation

Put all the solid ingredients into the Tall Cup and press them down below the Max Line. Add the fluid base to fill the cup up to the Max Line. Screw the Nutribullet Extractor Blade on to the top of the cup. Invert the cup, press it down into the Nutribullet Power Base and twist it into place. Blast the mixture until it is really smooth (20 or so seconds). **Enjoy!**

Blackberry and Tomato Regatta

Ingredients

1 Cup/Handful of Spinach (40 grams or 1½ oz)
1 Cup/Handful of Swiss Chard (40 grams or 1½ oz)
½ Cup of Blackberries (60 grams or 2 oz)
1 Cup/Handful of sliced Tomato (120 grams or 4 oz)
150 ml / 5 fl oz of Almond Milk (Unsweetened)

Protein 4g, Fat 2g, Carb 7g, Fibre 7g, 83 Kcals

Preparation

Put all the solid ingredients into the Tall Cup and press them down below the Max Line. Add the fluid base to fill the cup up to the Max Line. Screw the Nutribullet Extractor Blade on to the top of the cup. Invert the cup, press it down into the Nutribullet Power Base and twist it into place. Blast the mixture until it is really smooth (20 or so seconds). **Enjoy!**

Veggie Tango

Ingredients

1 Cup/Handful of Broccoli Florets (40 grams or 1½ oz)
1 Cup/Handful of Swiss Chard (40 grams or 1½ oz)
½ Cup of Blackberries (60 grams or 2 oz)
1 Cup/Handful of sliced Asparagus (120 grams or 4 oz)
150 ml / 5 fl oz of Almond Milk (Unsweetened)

Protein 6g, Fat 2g, Carb 7g, Fibre 8g, 90 Kcals

Preparation

Put all the solid ingredients into the Tall Cup and press them down below the Max Line. Add the fluid base to fill the cup up to the Max Line. Screw the Nutribullet Extractor Blade on to the top of the cup. Invert the cup, press it down into the Nutribullet Power Base and twist it into place. Blast the mixture until it is really smooth (20 or so seconds). **Enjoy!**

Broccoli embraces Chard

Ingredients

1 Cup/Handful of Broccoli Florets (40 grams or 1½ oz)
1 Cup/Handful of Swiss Chard (40 grams or 1½ oz)
½ Cup of Blackberries (60 grams or 2 oz)
1 Cup/Handful of sliced Tomato (120 grams or 4 oz)
150 ml / 5 fl oz of Almond Milk (Unsweetened)

Protein 4g, Fat 2g, Carb 8g, Fibre 7g, 88 Kcals

Preparation

Put all the solid ingredients into the Tall Cup and press them down below the Max Line. Add the fluid base to fill the cup up to the Max Line. Screw the Nutribullet Extractor Blade on to the top of the cup. Invert the cup, press it down into the Nutribullet Power Base and twist it into place. Blast the mixture until it is really smooth (20 or so seconds). **Enjoy!**

Black Kale loves Raspberry

Ingredients

1 Cup/Handful of Black Kale de-stemmed (40 grams or 1½ oz)
1 Cup/Handful of Broccoli Florets (40 grams or 1½ oz)
½ Cup of Raspberries (60 grams or 2 oz)
1 Cup/Handful of sliced Tomato (120 grams or 4 oz)
150 ml / 5 fl oz of Almond Milk (Unsweetened)

Protein 5g, Fat 3g, Carb 9g, Fibre 8g, 99 Kcals

Preparation

Put all the solid ingredients into the Tall Cup and press them down below the Max Line. Add the fluid base to fill the cup up to the Max Line. Screw the Nutribullet Extractor Blade on to the top of the cup. Invert the cup, press it down into the Nutribullet Power Base and twist it into place. Blast the mixture until it is really smooth (20 or so seconds). **Enjoy!**

Apricot joins Asparagus

Ingredients

2 Cups/Handfuls of Spinach (80 grams or 3 oz)
½ Cup of Apricot halves (60 grams or 2 oz)
1 Cup/Handful of sliced Asparagus (120 grams or 4 oz)
150 ml / 5 fl oz of Almond Milk (Unsweetened)

Protein 6g, Fat 2g, Carb 9g, Fibre 6g, 90 Kcals

Preparation

Put all the solid ingredients into the Tall Cup and press them down below the Max Line. Add the fluid base to fill the cup up to the Max Line. Screw the Nutribullet Extractor Blade on to the top of the cup. Invert the cup, press it down into the Nutribullet Power Base and twist it into place. Blast the mixture until it is really smooth (20 or so seconds). **Enjoy!**

Spinach goes Broccoli

Ingredients

1 Cup/Handful of Spinach (40 grams or 1½ oz)
1 Cup/Handful of Broccoli Florets (40 grams or 1½ oz)
½ Cup of Guava (60 grams or 2 oz)
1 Cup/Handful of sliced Asparagus (120 grams or 4 oz)
150 ml / 5 fl oz of Almond Milk (Unsweetened)

Protein 7g, Fat 3g, Carb 10g, Fibre 8g, 107 Kcals

Preparation

Put all the solid ingredients into the Tall Cup and press them down below the Max Line. Add the fluid base to fill the cup up to the Max Line. Screw the Nutribullet Extractor Blade on to the top of the cup. Invert the cup, press it down into the Nutribullet Power Base and twist it into place. Blast the mixture until it is really smooth (20 or so seconds). **Enjoy!**

Guava on Tomato

Ingredients

1 Cup/Handful of Black Kale de-stemmed (40 grams or 1½ oz)
1 Cup/Handful of Spinach (40 grams or 1½ oz)
½ Cup of Guava (60 grams or 2 oz)
1 Cup/Handful of sliced Tomato (120 grams or 4 oz)
150 ml / 5 fl oz of Almond Milk (Unsweetened)

Protein 6g, Fat 3g, Carb 10g, Fibre 7g, 105 Kcals

Preparation

Put all the solid ingredients into the Tall Cup and press them down below the Max Line. Add the fluid base to fill the cup up to the Max Line. Screw the Nutribullet Extractor Blade on to the top of the cup. Invert the cup, press it down into the Nutribullet Power Base and twist it into place. Blast the mixture until it is really smooth (20 or so seconds). **Enjoy!**

Papaya needs Tomato

Ingredients

1 Cup/Handful of Spinach (40 grams or 1½ oz)
1 Cup/Handful of Black Kale de-stemmed (40 grams or 1½ oz)
½ Cup of Papaya (60 grams or 2 oz)
1 Cup/Handful of sliced Tomato (120 grams or 4 oz)
150 ml / 5 fl oz of Almond Milk (Unsweetened)

Protein 4g, Fat 3g, Carb 10g, Fibre 5g, 90 Kcals

Preparation

Put all the solid ingredients into the Tall Cup and press them down below the Max Line. Add the fluid base to fill the cup up to the Max Line. Screw the Nutribullet Extractor Blade on to the top of the cup. Invert the cup, press it down into the Nutribullet Power Base and twist it into place. Blast the mixture until it is really smooth (20 or so seconds). **Enjoy!**

Apricot goes Tomato

Ingredients

1 Cup/Handful of Spinach (40 grams or 1½ oz)
1 Cup/Handful of Black Kale de-stemmed (40 grams or 1½ oz)
½ Cup of Apricot halves (60 grams or 2 oz)
1 Cup/Handful of sliced Tomato (120 grams or 4 oz)
150 ml / 5 fl oz of Almond Milk (Unsweetened)

Protein 5g, Fat 3g, Carb 10g, Fibre 5g, 93 Kcals

Preparation

Put all the solid ingredients into the Tall Cup and press them down below the Max Line. Add the fluid base to fill the cup up to the Max Line. Screw the Nutribullet Extractor Blade on to the top of the cup. Invert the cup, press it down into the Nutribullet Power Base and twist it into place. Blast the mixture until it is really smooth (20 or so seconds). **Enjoy!**

Beetroot Blossom

Ingredients

1 Cup/Handful of Swiss Chard (40 grams or 1½ oz)
1 Cup/Handful of Spinach (40 grams or 1½ oz)
½ Cup of Avocado slices (60 grams or 2 oz)
1 Cup/Handful of diced Beetroot (120 grams or 4 oz)
150 ml / 5 fl oz of Almond Milk (Unsweetened)

Protein 6g, Fat 11g, Carb 11g, Fibre 10g, 183 Kcals

Preparation

Put all the solid ingredients into the Tall Cup and press them down below the Max Line. Add the fluid base to fill the cup up to the Max Line. Screw the Nutribullet Extractor Blade on to the top of the cup. Invert the cup, press it down into the Nutribullet Power Base and twist it into place. Blast the mixture until it is really smooth (20 or so seconds). *Enjoy!*

Blueberry loves Asparagus

Ingredients

1 Cup/Handful of Spinach (40 grams or 1½ oz)
1 Cup/Handful of Black Kale de-stemmed (40 grams or 1½ oz)
½ Cup of Blueberries (60 grams or 2 oz)
1 Cup/Handful of sliced Asparagus (120 grams or 4 oz)
150 ml / 5 fl oz of Almond Milk (Unsweetened)

Protein 6g, Fat 3g, Carb 11g, Fibre 6g, 100 Kcals

Preparation

Put all the solid ingredients into the Tall Cup and press them down below the Max Line. Add the fluid base to fill the cup up to the Max Line. Screw the Nutribullet Extractor Blade on to the top of the cup. Invert the cup, press it down into the Nutribullet Power Base and twist it into place. Blast the mixture until it is really smooth (20 or so seconds). *Enjoy!*

Carrot Crush

Ingredients

1 Cup/Handful of Swiss Chard (40 grams or 1½ oz)
1 Cup/Handful of Black Kale de-stemmed (40 grams or 1½ oz)
½ Cup of Avocado slices (60 grams or 2 oz)
1 Cup/Handful of sliced Carrots (120 grams or 4 oz)
150 ml / 5 fl oz of Almond Milk (Unsweetened)

Protein 5g, Fat 11g, Carb 11g, Fibre 10g, 186 Kcals

Preparation

Put all the solid ingredients into the Tall Cup and press them down below the Max Line. Add the fluid base to fill the cup up to the Max Line. Screw the Nutribullet Extractor Blade on to the top of the cup. Invert the cup, press it down into the Nutribullet Power Base and twist it into place. Blast the mixture until it is really smooth (20 or so seconds). *Enjoy!*

Happiness and Deep Sleep Blasts
High in Tryptophan, Magnesium,. Vits B3, B6, B9

Veggie Smash

Ingredients

1 Cup/Handful of Watercress (40 grams or 1½ oz)
1 Cup/Handful of Broccoli Florets (40 grams or 1½ oz)
½ Cup of Avocado slices (60 grams or 2 oz)
1 Cup/Handful of sliced Fine Beans (120 grams or 4 oz)
22 grams or ¾ oz of Sesame Seeds Hulled
150 ml / 5 fl oz of Almond Milk (Unsweetened)

Protein 10g, Fat 24g, Carb 7g, Fibre 10g, 295 Kcals

Preparation

Place the nuts or seeds into the Tall Cup. Screw the Nutribullet Extractor Blade on to the top of the cup. Invert the cup, press it down into the Nutribullet Power Base and twist it into place. Blast them for 30 seconds. Put the rest of the solid ingredients into the cup and press them down below the Max Line. Add the fluid base to fill the cup up to the Max Line. Screw the Nutribullet Extractor Blade on to the top of the cup. Invert the cup, press it down into the Nutribullet Power Base and twist it into place. Blast the mixture until it is really smooth (20 or so seconds). *Enjoy!*

Broccoli and Spinach Reaction

Ingredients

1 Cup/Handful of Broccoli Florets (40 grams or 1½ oz)
1 Cup/Handful of Spinach (40 grams or 1½ oz)
½ Cup of Avocado slices (60 grams or 2 oz)
1 Cup/Handful of sliced Fine Beans (120 grams or 4 oz)
22 grams or ¾ oz of Sesame Seeds Hulled
150 ml / 5 fl oz of Almond Milk (Unsweetened)

Protein 10g, Fat 24g, Carb 7g, Fibre 11g, 299 Kcals

Preparation

Place the nuts or seeds into the Tall Cup. Screw the Nutribullet Extractor Blade on to the top of the cup. Invert the cup, press it down into the Nutribullet Power Base and twist it into place. Blast them for 30 seconds. Put the rest of the solid ingredients into the cup and press them down below the Max Line. Add the fluid base to fill the cup up to the Max Line. Screw the Nutribullet Extractor Blade on to the top of the cup. Invert the cup, press it down into the Nutribullet Power Base and twist it into place. Blast the mixture until it is really smooth (20 or so seconds). ***Enjoy!***

Watercress and Avocado Invigorator

Ingredients

1 Cup/Handful of Watercress (40 grams or 1½ oz)
1 Cup/Handful of Spinach (40 grams or 1½ oz)
½ Cup of Avocado slices (60 grams or 2 oz)
1 Cup/Handful of sliced Fine Beans (120 grams or 4 oz)
22 grams or ¾ oz of Pumpkin Seeds
150 ml / 5 fl oz of Almond Milk (Unsweetened)

Protein 11g, Fat 21g, Carb 8g, Fibre 10g, 283 Kcals

Preparation

Place the nuts or seeds into the Tall Cup. Screw the Nutribullet Extractor Blade on to the top of the cup. Invert the cup, press it down into the Nutribullet Power Base and twist it into place. Blast them for 30 seconds. Put the rest of the solid ingredients into the cup and press them down below the Max Line. Add the fluid base to fill the cup up to the Max Line. Screw the Nutribullet Extractor Blade on to the top of the cup. Invert the cup, press it down into the Nutribullet Power Base and twist it into place. Blast the mixture until it is really smooth (20 or so seconds). ***Enjoy!***

Veggie Ensemble

Ingredients

2 Cups/Handfuls of Spinach (80 grams or 3 oz)
½ Cup of Avocado slices (60 grams or 2 oz)
1 Cup/Handful of sliced Cauliflower florets (120 grams or 4 oz)
30 grams or 1 oz of Peanuts
150 ml / 5 fl oz of Almond Milk (Unsweetened)

Protein 14g, Fat 26g, Carb 8g, Fibre 11g, 334 Kcals

Preparation

Place the nuts or seeds into the Tall Cup. Screw the Nutribullet Extractor Blade on to the top of the cup. Invert the cup, press it down into the Nutribullet Power Base and twist it into place. Blast them for 30 seconds. Put the rest of the solid ingredients into the cup and press them down below the Max Line. Add the fluid base to fill the cup up to the Max Line. Screw the Nutribullet Extractor Blade on to the top of the cup. Invert the cup, press it down into the Nutribullet Power Base and twist it into place. Blast the mixture until it is really smooth (20 or so seconds). **Enjoy!**

Sunflower Sunrise

Ingredients

2 Cups/Handfuls of Watercress (80 grams or 3 oz)
½ Cup of Avocado slices (60 grams or 2 oz)
1 Cup/Handful of sliced Fine Beans (120 grams or 4 oz)
22 grams or ¾ oz of Sunflower Seeds Hulled
150 ml / 5 fl oz of Almond Milk (Unsweetened)

Protein 10g, Fat 22g, Carb 8g, Fibre 9g, 268 Kcals

Preparation

Place the nuts or seeds into the Tall Cup. Screw the Nutribullet Extractor Blade on to the top of the cup. Invert the cup, press it down into the Nutribullet Power Base and twist it into place. Blast them for 30 seconds. Put the rest of the solid ingredients into the cup and press them down below the Max Line. Add the fluid base to fill the cup up to the Max Line. Screw the Nutribullet Extractor Blade on to the top of the cup. Invert the cup, press it down into the Nutribullet Power Base and twist it into place. Blast the mixture until it is really smooth (20 or so seconds). **Enjoy!**

Fruity Delusion

Ingredients

1 Cup/Handful of Spinach (40 grams or 1½ oz)
1 Cup/Handful of Broccoli Florets (40 grams or 1½ oz)
½ Cup of Avocado slices (60 grams or 2 oz)
1 Cup/Handful of sliced Cauliflower florets (120 grams or 4 oz)
22 grams or ¾ oz of Chia Seeds
150 ml / 5 fl oz of Almond Milk (Unsweetened)

Protein 10g, Fat 18g, Carb 9g, Fibre 17g, 275 Kcals

Preparation

Place the nuts or seeds into the Tall Cup. Screw the Nutribullet Extractor Blade on to the top of the cup. Invert the cup, press it down into the Nutribullet Power Base and twist it into place. Blast them for 30 seconds. Put the rest of the solid ingredients into the cup and press them down below the Max Line. Add the fluid base to fill the cup up to the Max Line. Screw the Nutribullet Extractor Blade on to the top of the cup. Invert the cup, press it down into the Nutribullet Power Base and twist it into place. Blast the mixture until it is really smooth (20 or so seconds). *Enjoy!*

Broccoli and Walnut Fusion

Ingredients

1 Cup/Handful of Broccoli Florets (40 grams or 1½ oz)
1 Cup/Handful of Watercress (40 grams or 1½ oz)
½ Cup of Avocado slices (60 grams or 2 oz)
1 Cup/Handful of sliced Cauliflower florets (120 grams or 4 oz)
30 grams or 1 oz of Walnuts
150 ml / 5 fl oz of Almond Milk (Unsweetened)

Protein 11g, Fat 31g, Carb 9g, Fibre 10g, 359 Kcals

Preparation

Place the nuts or seeds into the Tall Cup. Screw the Nutribullet Extractor Blade on to the top of the cup. Invert the cup, press it down into the Nutribullet Power Base and twist it into place. Blast them for 30 seconds. Put the rest of the solid ingredients into the cup and press them down below the Max Line. Add the fluid base to fill the cup up to the Max Line. Screw the Nutribullet Extractor Blade on to the top of the cup. Invert the cup, press it down into the Nutribullet Power Base and twist it into place. Blast the mixture until it is really smooth (20 or so seconds). *Enjoy!*

Fruity Utopia

Ingredients

2 Cups/Handfuls of Broccoli Florets (80 grams or 3 oz)
½ Cup of Avocado slices (60 grams or 2 oz)
1 Cup/Handful of sliced Fine Beans (120 grams or 4 oz)
22 grams or ¾ oz of Pumpkin Seeds
150 ml / 5 fl oz of Almond Milk (Unsweetened)

Protein 12g, Fat 21g, Carb 10g, Fibre 11g, 297 Kcals

Preparation

Place the nuts or seeds into the Tall Cup. Screw the Nutribullet Extractor Blade on to the top of the cup. Invert the cup, press it down into the Nutribullet Power Base and twist it into place. Blast them for 30 seconds. Put the rest of the solid ingredients into the cup and press them down below the Max Line. Add the fluid base to fill the cup up to the Max Line. Screw the Nutribullet Extractor Blade on to the top of the cup. Invert the cup, press it down into the Nutribullet Power Base and twist it into place. Blast the mixture until it is really smooth (20 or so seconds). **Enjoy!**

Veggie Cocktail

Ingredients

1 Cup/Handful of Watercress (40 grams or 1½ oz)
1 Cup/Handful of Spinach (40 grams or 1½ oz)
½ Cup of Avocado slices (60 grams or 2 oz)
1 Cup/Handful of diced Beetroot (120 grams or 4 oz)
22 grams or ¾ oz of Sesame Seeds Hulled
150 ml / 5 fl oz of Almond Milk (Unsweetened)

Protein 10g, Fat 24g, Carb 10g, Fibre 11g, 312 Kcals

Preparation

Place the nuts or seeds into the Tall Cup. Screw the Nutribullet Extractor Blade on to the top of the cup. Invert the cup, press it down into the Nutribullet Power Base and twist it into place. Blast them for 30 seconds. Put the rest of the solid ingredients into the cup and press them down below the Max Line. Add the fluid base to fill the cup up to the Max Line. Screw the Nutribullet Extractor Blade on to the top of the cup. Invert the cup, press it down into the Nutribullet Power Base and twist it into place. Blast the mixture until it is really smooth (20 or so seconds). **Enjoy!**

Broccoli and Sunflower Salad

Ingredients

2 Cups/Handfuls of Broccoli Florets (80 grams or 3 oz)
½ Cup of Avocado slices (60 grams or 2 oz)
1 Cup/Handful of sliced Cauliflower florets (120 grams or 4 oz)
22 grams or ¾ oz of Sunflower Seeds Hulled
150 ml / 5 fl oz of Almond Milk (Unsweetened)

Protein 11g, Fat 22g, Carb 11g, Fibre 10g, 286 Kcals

Preparation

Place the nuts or seeds into the Tall Cup. Screw the Nutribullet Extractor Blade on to the top of the cup. Invert the cup, press it down into the Nutribullet Power Base and twist it into place. Blast them for 30 seconds. Put the rest of the solid ingredients into the cup and press them down below the Max Line. Add the fluid base to fill the cup up to the Max Line. Screw the Nutribullet Extractor Blade on to the top of the cup. Invert the cup, press it down into the Nutribullet Power Base and twist it into place. Blast the mixture until it is really smooth (20 or so seconds). **Enjoy!**

Heart Care Blasts
Anti-inflammatory, high in Omega 3, anti oxidants, Vitamins C, E

Black Kale and Blackberry Power

Ingredients

2 Cups/Handfuls of Black Kale de-stemmed (80 grams or 3 oz)
½ Cup of Blackberries (60 grams or 2 oz)
1 Cup/Handful of sliced Asparagus (120 grams or 4 oz)
22 grams or ¾ oz of Sesame Seeds Hulled
150 ml / 5 fl oz of Almond Milk (Unsweetened)

Protein 11g, Fat 16g, Carb 7g, Fibre 10g, 228 Kcals

Preparation

Place the nuts or seeds into the Tall Cup. Screw the Nutribullet Extractor Blade on to the top of the cup. Invert the cup, press it down into the Nutribullet Power Base and twist it into place. Blast them for 30 seconds. Put the rest of the solid ingredients into the cup and press them down below the Max Line. Add the fluid base to fill the cup up to the Max Line. Screw the Nutribullet Extractor Blade on to the top of the cup. Invert the cup, press it down into the Nutribullet Power Base and twist it into place. Blast the mixture until it is really smooth (20 or so seconds). **Enjoy!**

Rocket loves Sesame

Ingredients

1 Cup/Handful of Rocket/Arugura Lettuce (40 grams or 1½ oz)
1 Cup/Handful of Lettuce Leaves (40 grams or 1½ oz)
½ Cup of Blackberries (60 grams or 2 oz)
1 Cup/Handful of sliced Cauliflower florets (120 grams or 4 oz)
22 grams or ¾ oz of Sesame Seeds Hulled
150 ml / 5 fl oz of Almond Milk (Unsweetened)

Protein 9g, Fat 15g, Carb 8g, Fibre 9g, 219 Kcals

Preparation

Place the nuts or seeds into the Tall Cup. Screw the Nutribullet Extractor Blade on to the top of the cup. Invert the cup, press it down into the Nutribullet Power Base and twist it into place. Blast them for 30 seconds. Put the rest of the solid ingredients into the cup and press them down below the Max Line. Add the fluid base to fill the cup up to the Max Line. Screw the Nutribullet Extractor Blade on to the top of the cup. Invert the cup, press it down into the Nutribullet Power Base and twist it into place. Blast the mixture until it is really smooth (20 or so seconds). **Enjoy!**

Rocket goes Blackberry

Ingredients

2 Cups/Handfuls of Rocket/Arugura Lettuce (80 grams or 3 oz)
½ Cup of Blackberries (60 grams or 2 oz)
1 Cup/Handful of sliced Cauliflower florets (120 grams or 4 oz)
22 grams or ¾ oz of Chia Seeds
150 ml / 5 fl oz of Almond Milk (Unsweetened)

Protein 8g, Fat 9g, Carb 9g, Fibre 15g, 194 Kcals

Preparation

Place the nuts or seeds into the Tall Cup. Screw the Nutribullet Extractor Blade on to the top of the cup. Invert the cup, press it down into the Nutribullet Power Base and twist it into place. Blast them for 30 seconds. Put the rest of the solid ingredients into the cup and press them down below the Max Line. Add the fluid base to fill the cup up to the Max Line. Screw the Nutribullet Extractor Blade on to the top of the cup. Invert the cup, press it down into the Nutribullet Power Base and twist it into place. Blast the mixture until it is really smooth (20 or so seconds). **Enjoy!**

Black Kale and Strawberry Revision

Ingredients

1 Cup/Handful of Black Kale de-stemmed (40 grams or 1½ oz)
1 Cup/Handful of Spinach (40 grams or 1½ oz)
½ Cup of Strawberries (60 grams or 2 oz)
1 Cup/Handful of sliced Tomato (120 grams or 4 oz)
22 grams or ¾ oz of Chia Seeds
150 ml / 5 fl oz of Almond Milk (Unsweetened)

Protein 8g, Fat 10g, Carb 10g, Fibre 13g, 190 Kcals

Preparation

Place the nuts or seeds into the Tall Cup. Screw the Nutribullet Extractor Blade on to the top of the cup. Invert the cup, press it down into the Nutribullet Power Base and twist it into place. Blast them for 30 seconds. Put the rest of the solid ingredients into the cup and press them down below the Max Line. Add the fluid base to fill the cup up to the Max Line. Screw the Nutribullet Extractor Blade on to the top of the cup. Invert the cup, press it down into the Nutribullet Power Base and twist it into place. Blast the mixture until it is really smooth (20 or so seconds). *Enjoy!*

Flax Fiesta

Ingredients

1 Cup/Handful of Black Kale de-stemmed (40 grams or 1½ oz)
1 Cup/Handful of Broccoli Florets (40 grams or 1½ oz)
½ Cup of Strawberries (60 grams or 2 oz)
1 Cup/Handful of sliced Cauliflower florets (120 grams or 4 oz)
22 grams or ¾ oz of Flax Seeds
150 ml / 5 fl oz of Almond Milk (Unsweetened)

Protein 10g, Fat 12g, Carb 10g, Fibre 12g, 213 Kcals

Preparation

Place the nuts or seeds into the Tall Cup. Screw the Nutribullet Extractor Blade on to the top of the cup. Invert the cup, press it down into the Nutribullet Power Base and twist it into place. Blast them for 30 seconds. Put the rest of the solid ingredients into the cup and press them down below the Max Line. Add the fluid base to fill the cup up to the Max Line. Screw the Nutribullet Extractor Blade on to the top of the cup. Invert the cup, press it down into the Nutribullet Power Base and twist it into place. Blast the mixture until it is really smooth (20 or so seconds). *Enjoy!*

Lettuce Lagoon

Ingredients

1 Cup/Handful of Spinach (40 grams or 1½ oz)
1 Cup/Handful of Lettuce Leaves (40 grams or 1½ oz)
½ Cup of Nectarine segments (60 grams or 2 oz)
1 Cup/Handful of sliced Tomato (120 grams or 4 oz)
22 grams or ¾ oz of Sesame Seeds Hulled
150 ml / 5 fl oz of Almond Milk (Unsweetened)

Protein 8g, Fat 15g, Carb 10g, Fibre 7g, 215 Kcals

Preparation

Place the nuts or seeds into the Tall Cup. Screw the Nutribullet Extractor Blade on to the top of the cup. Invert the cup, press it down into the Nutribullet Power Base and twist it into place. Blast them for 30 seconds. Put the rest of the solid ingredients into the cup and press them down below the Max Line. Add the fluid base to fill the cup up to the Max Line. Screw the Nutribullet Extractor Blade on to the top of the cup. Invert the cup, press it down into the Nutribullet Power Base and twist it into place. Blast the mixture until it is really smooth (20 or so seconds). **Enjoy!**

Nectarine Nectar

Ingredients

2 Cups/Handfuls of Lettuce Leaves (80 grams or 3 oz)
½ Cup of Nectarine segments (60 grams or 2 oz)
1 Cup/Handful of sliced Asparagus (120 grams or 4 oz)
22 grams or ¾ oz of Chia Seeds
150 ml / 5 fl oz of Almond Milk (Unsweetened)

Protein 8g, Fat 9g, Carb 10g, Fibre 13g, 190 Kcals

Preparation

Place the nuts or seeds into the Tall Cup. Screw the Nutribullet Extractor Blade on to the top of the cup. Invert the cup, press it down into the Nutribullet Power Base and twist it into place. Blast them for 30 seconds. Put the rest of the solid ingredients into the cup and press them down below the Max Line. Add the fluid base to fill the cup up to the Max Line. Screw the Nutribullet Extractor Blade on to the top of the cup. Invert the cup, press it down into the Nutribullet Power Base and twist it into place. Blast the mixture until it is really smooth (20 or so seconds). **Enjoy!**

Pecan Presented

Ingredients

1 Cup/Handful of Lettuce Leaves (40 grams or 1½ oz)
1 Cup/Handful of Black Kale de-stemmed (40 grams or 1½ oz)
½ Cup of Raspberries (60 grams or 2 oz)
1 Cup/Handful of sliced Red Pepper (120 grams or 4 oz)
30 grams or 1 oz of Pecans
150 ml / 5 fl oz of Almond Milk (Unsweetened)

Protein 7g, Fat 25g, Carb 11g, Fibre 12g, 315 Kcals

Preparation

Place the nuts or seeds into the Tall Cup. Screw the Nutribullet Extractor Blade on to the top of the cup. Invert the cup, press it down into the Nutribullet Power Base and twist it into place. Blast them for 30 seconds. Put the rest of the solid ingredients into the cup and press them down below the Max Line. Add the fluid base to fill the cup up to the Max Line. Screw the Nutribullet Extractor Blade on to the top of the cup. Invert the cup, press it down into the Nutribullet Power Base and twist it into place. Blast the mixture until it is really smooth (20 or so seconds). *Enjoy!*

Orange Orchestra

Ingredients

2 Cups/Handfuls of Spinach (80 grams or 3 oz)
½ Cup of Orange segments (60 grams or 2 oz)
1 Cup/Handful of sliced Asparagus (120 grams or 4 oz)
22 grams or ¾ oz of Chia Seeds
150 ml / 5 fl oz of Almond Milk (Unsweetened)

Protein 10g, Fat 9g, Carb 11g, Fibre 14g, 197 Kcals

Preparation

Place the nuts or seeds into the Tall Cup. Screw the Nutribullet Extractor Blade on to the top of the cup. Invert the cup, press it down into the Nutribullet Power Base and twist it into place. Blast them for 30 seconds. Put the rest of the solid ingredients into the cup and press them down below the Max Line. Add the fluid base to fill the cup up to the Max Line. Screw the Nutribullet Extractor Blade on to the top of the cup. Invert the cup, press it down into the Nutribullet Power Base and twist it into place. Blast the mixture until it is really smooth (20 or so seconds). *Enjoy!*

Red Pepper Rush

Ingredients

1 Cup/Handful of Rocket/Arugura Lettuce (40 grams or 1½ oz)
1 Cup/Handful of Broccoli Florets (40 grams or 1½ oz)
½ Cup of Blackberries (60 grams or 2 oz)
1 Cup/Handful of sliced Red Pepper (120 grams or 4 oz)
30 grams or 1 oz of Pecans
150 ml / 5 fl oz of Almond Milk (Unsweetened)

Protein 7g, Fat 24g, Carb 11g, Fibre 11g, 309 Kcals

Preparation

Place the nuts or seeds into the Tall Cup. Screw the Nutribullet Extractor Blade on to the top of the cup. Invert the cup, press it down into the Nutribullet Power Base and twist it into place. Blast them for 30 seconds. Put the rest of the solid ingredients into the cup and press them down below the Max Line. Add the fluid base to fill the cup up to the Max Line. Screw the Nutribullet Extractor Blade on to the top of the cup. Invert the cup, press it down into the Nutribullet Power Base and twist it into place. Blast the mixture until it is really smooth (20 or so seconds). **Enjoy!**

Detoxing and Cleansing Blasts
All ingredients have detoxing capabilities (With Carb Grams)

Avocado joins Asparagus

Ingredients

2 Cups/Handfuls of Fennel (80 grams or 3 oz)
½ Cup of Avocado slices (60 grams or 2 oz)
1 Cup/Handful of sliced Asparagus (120 grams or 4 oz)
22 grams or ¾ oz of Sesame Seeds Hulled
150 ml / 5 fl oz of Almond Milk (Unsweetened)

Protein 9g, Fat 24g, Carb 7g, Fibre 11g, 295 Kcals

Preparation

Place the nuts or seeds into the Tall Cup. Screw the Nutribullet Extractor Blade on to the top of the cup. Invert the cup, press it down into the Nutribullet Power Base and twist it into place. Blast them for 30 seconds. Put the rest of the solid ingredients into the cup and press them down below the Max Line. Add the fluid base to fill the cup up to the Max Line. Screw the Nutribullet Extractor Blade on to the top of the cup. Invert the cup, press it down into the Nutribullet Power Base and twist it into place. Blast the mixture until it is really smooth (20 or so seconds). **Enjoy!**

Green Cabbage meets Brazil

Ingredients

2 Cups/Handfuls of Green Cabbage (80 grams or 3 oz)
½ Cup of Avocado slices (60 grams or 2 oz)
1 Cup/Handful of sliced Asparagus (120 grams or 4 oz)
30 grams or 1 oz of Brazil nuts
150 ml / 5 fl oz of Almond Milk (Unsweetened)

Protein 10g, Fat 31g, Carb 7g, Fibre 11g, 357 Kcals

Preparation

Place the nuts or seeds into the Tall Cup. Screw the Nutribullet Extractor Blade on to the top of the cup. Invert the cup, press it down into the Nutribullet Power Base and twist it into place. Blast them for 30 seconds. Put the rest of the solid ingredients into the cup and press them down below the Max Line. Add the fluid base to fill the cup up to the Max Line. Screw the Nutribullet Extractor Blade on to the top of the cup. Invert the cup, press it down into the Nutribullet Power Base and twist it into place. Blast the mixture until it is really smooth (20 or so seconds). *Enjoy!*

Green Cabbage and Grapefruit Wonder

Ingredients

1 Cup/Handful of Green Cabbage (40 grams or 1½ oz)
1 Cup/Handful of Watercress (40 grams or 1½ oz)
½ Cup of Grapefruit segments (60 grams or 2 oz)
1 Cup/Handful of sliced Asparagus (120 grams or 4 oz)
22 grams or ¾ oz of Sesame Seeds Hulled
150 ml / 5 fl oz of Almond Milk (Unsweetened)

Protein 9g, Fat 15g, Carb 8g, Fibre 7g, 208 Kcals

Preparation

Place the nuts or seeds into the Tall Cup. Screw the Nutribullet Extractor Blade on to the top of the cup. Invert the cup, press it down into the Nutribullet Power Base and twist it into place. Blast them for 30 seconds. Put the rest of the solid ingredients into the cup and press them down below the Max Line. Add the fluid base to fill the cup up to the Max Line. Screw the Nutribullet Extractor Blade on to the top of the cup. Invert the cup, press it down into the Nutribullet Power Base and twist it into place. Blast the mixture until it is really smooth (20 or so seconds). *Enjoy!*

Grapefruit Gala

Ingredients

1 Cup/Handful of Black Kale de-stemmed (40 grams or 1½ oz)
1 Cup/Handful of Broccoli Florets (40 grams or 1½ oz)
½ Cup of Grapefruit segments (60 grams or 2 oz)
1 Cup/Handful of sliced Asparagus (120 grams or 4 oz)
22 grams or ¾ oz of Sesame Seeds Hulled
150 ml / 5 fl oz of Almond Milk (Unsweetened)

Protein 10g, Fat 15g, Carb 9g, Fibre 7g, 221 Kcals

Preparation

Place the nuts or seeds into the Tall Cup. Screw the Nutribullet Extractor Blade on to the top of the cup. Invert the cup, press it down into the Nutribullet Power Base and twist it into place. Blast them for 30 seconds. Put the rest of the solid ingredients into the cup and press them down below the Max Line. Add the fluid base to fill the cup up to the Max Line. Screw the Nutribullet Extractor Blade on to the top of the cup. Invert the cup, press it down into the Nutribullet Power Base and twist it into place. Blast the mixture until it is really smooth (20 or so seconds). **Enjoy!**

Watercress Waterfall

Ingredients

1 Cup/Handful of Broccoli Florets (40 grams or 1½ oz)
1 Cup/Handful of Watercress (40 grams or 1½ oz)
½ Cup of Grapefruit segments (60 grams or 2 oz)
1 Cup/Handful of sliced Asparagus (120 grams or 4 oz)
30 grams or 1 oz of Brazil nuts
150 ml / 5 fl oz of Almond Milk (Unsweetened)

Protein 10g, Fat 22g, Carb 10g, Fibre 7g, 278 Kcals

Preparation

Place the nuts or seeds into the Tall Cup. Screw the Nutribullet Extractor Blade on to the top of the cup. Invert the cup, press it down into the Nutribullet Power Base and twist it into place. Blast them for 30 seconds. Put the rest of the solid ingredients into the cup and press them down below the Max Line. Add the fluid base to fill the cup up to the Max Line. Screw the Nutribullet Extractor Blade on to the top of the cup. Invert the cup, press it down into the Nutribullet Power Base and twist it into place. Blast the mixture until it is really smooth (20 or so seconds). **Enjoy!**

Grapefruit and Asparagus Potion

Ingredients

1 Cup/Handful of Broccoli Florets (40 grams or 1½ oz)
1 Cup/Handful of Fennel (40 grams or 1½ oz)
½ Cup of Grapefruit segments (60 grams or 2 oz)
1 Cup/Handful of sliced Asparagus (120 grams or 4 oz)
22 grams or ¾ oz of Sesame Seeds Hulled
150 ml / 5 fl oz of Almond Milk (Unsweetened)

Protein 9g, Fat 15g, Carb 10g, Fibre 8g, 220 Kcals

Preparation

Place the nuts or seeds into the Tall Cup. Screw the Nutribullet Extractor Blade on to the top of the cup. Invert the cup, press it down into the Nutribullet Power Base and twist it into place. Blast them for 30 seconds. Put the rest of the solid ingredients into the cup and press them down below the Max Line. Add the fluid base to fill the cup up to the Max Line. Screw the Nutribullet Extractor Blade on to the top of the cup. Invert the cup, press it down into the Nutribullet Power Base and twist it into place. Blast the mixture until it is really smooth (20 or so seconds). **Enjoy!**

Red Cabbage and Sesame Symphony

Ingredients

1 Cup/Handful of Red or White Cabbage (40 grams or 1½ oz)
1 Cup/Handful of Green Cabbage (40 grams or 1½ oz)
½ Cup of Grapefruit segments (60 grams or 2 oz)
1 Cup/Handful of sliced Asparagus (120 grams or 4 oz)
22 grams or ¾ oz of Sesame Seeds Hulled
150 ml / 5 fl oz of Almond Milk (Unsweetened)

Protein 9g, Fat 15g, Carb 10g, Fibre 7g, 216 Kcals

Preparation

Place the nuts or seeds into the Tall Cup. Screw the Nutribullet Extractor Blade on to the top of the cup. Invert the cup, press it down into the Nutribullet Power Base and twist it into place. Blast them for 30 seconds. Put the rest of the solid ingredients into the cup and press them down below the Max Line. Add the fluid base to fill the cup up to the Max Line. Screw the Nutribullet Extractor Blade on to the top of the cup. Invert the cup, press it down into the Nutribullet Power Base and twist it into place. Blast the mixture until it is really smooth (20 or so seconds). **Enjoy!**

Grapefruit embraces Asparagus

Ingredients

1 Cup/Handful of Watercress (40 grams or 1½ oz)
1 Cup/Handful of Red or White Cabbage (40 grams or 1½ oz)
½ Cup of Grapefruit segments (60 grams or 2 oz)
1 Cup/Handful of sliced Asparagus (120 grams or 4 oz)
30 grams or 1 oz of Brazil nuts
150 ml / 5 fl oz of Almond Milk (Unsweetened)

Protein 9g, Fat 22g, Carb 10g, Fibre 7g, 277 Kcals

Preparation

Place the nuts or seeds into the Tall Cup. Screw the Nutribullet Extractor Blade on to the top of the cup. Invert the cup, press it down into the Nutribullet Power Base and twist it into place. Blast them for 30 seconds. Put the rest of the solid ingredients into the cup and press them down below the Max Line. Add the fluid base to fill the cup up to the Max Line. Screw the Nutribullet Extractor Blade on to the top of the cup. Invert the cup, press it down into the Nutribullet Power Base and twist it into place. Blast the mixture until it is really smooth (20 or so seconds). *Enjoy!*

Watercress and Pineapple Delivered

Ingredients

1 Cup/Handful of Watercress (40 grams or 1½ oz)
1 Cup/Handful of Black Kale de-stemmed (40 grams or 1½ oz)
½ Cup of Pineapple chunks (60 grams or 2 oz)
1 Cup/Handful of sliced Asparagus (120 grams or 4 oz)
22 grams or ¾ oz of Sesame Seeds Hulled
150 ml / 5 fl oz of Almond Milk (Unsweetened)

Protein 10g, Fat 15g, Carb 11g, Fibre 7g, 223 Kcals

Preparation

Place the nuts or seeds into the Tall Cup. Screw the Nutribullet Extractor Blade on to the top of the cup. Invert the cup, press it down into the Nutribullet Power Base and twist it into place. Blast them for 30 seconds. Put the rest of the solid ingredients into the cup and press them down below the Max Line. Add the fluid base to fill the cup up to the Max Line. Screw the Nutribullet Extractor Blade on to the top of the cup. Invert the cup, press it down into the Nutribullet Power Base and twist it into place. Blast the mixture until it is really smooth (20 or so seconds). *Enjoy!*

Fennel and Brazil Breeze

Ingredients

1 Cup/Handful of Green Cabbage (40 grams or 1½ oz)
1 Cup/Handful of Fennel (40 grams or 1½ oz)
½ Cup of Grapefruit segments (60 grams or 2 oz)
1 Cup/Handful of sliced Asparagus (120 grams or 4 oz)
30 grams or 1 oz of Brazil nuts
150 ml / 5 fl oz of Almond Milk (Unsweetened)

Protein 9g, Fat 22g, Carb 11g, Fibre 8g, 282 Kcals

Preparation

Place the nuts or seeds into the Tall Cup. Screw the Nutribullet Extractor Blade on to the top of the cup. Invert the cup, press it down into the Nutribullet Power Base and twist it into place. Blast them for 30 seconds. Put the rest of the solid ingredients into the cup and press them down below the Max Line. Add the fluid base to fill the cup up to the Max Line. Screw the Nutribullet Extractor Blade on to the top of the cup. Invert the cup, press it down into the Nutribullet Power Base and twist it into place. Blast the mixture until it is really smooth (20 or so seconds). *Enjoy!*

Clear Thinking Brain Food Blasts
High in Omega3, Beta Carotene, Lycopene, Magnesium, Zinc, Vitamins B, C, E

Blackberry needs Flax

Ingredients

1 Cup/Handful of Bok Choy (40 grams or 1½ oz)
1 Cup/Handful of Spinach (40 grams or 1½ oz)
½ Cup of Blackberries (60 grams or 2 oz)
1 Cup/Handful of sliced Tomato (120 grams or 4 oz)
22 grams or ¾ oz of Flax Seeds
150 ml / 5 fl oz of Almond Milk (Unsweetened)

Protein 8g, Fat 12g, Carb 7g, Fibre 13g, 198 Kcals

Preparation

Place the nuts or seeds into the Tall Cup. Screw the Nutribullet Extractor Blade on to the top of the cup. Invert the cup, press it down into the Nutribullet Power Base and twist it into place. Blast them for 30 seconds. Put the rest of the solid ingredients into the cup and press them down below the Max Line. Add the fluid base to fill the cup up to the Max Line. Screw the Nutribullet Extractor Blade on to the top of the cup. Invert the cup, press it down into the Nutribullet Power Base and twist it into place. Blast the mixture until it is really smooth (20 or so seconds). *Enjoy!*

Bok Choy and Almond Surprise

Ingredients

2 Cups/Handfuls of Bok Choy (80 grams or 3 oz)
½ Cup of Blackberries (60 grams or 2 oz)
1 Cup/Handful of sliced Tomato (120 grams or 4 oz)
30 grams or 1 oz of Almonds
150 ml / 5 fl oz of Almond Milk (Unsweetened)

Protein 10g, Fat 18g, Carb 9g, Fibre 9g, 254 Kcals

Preparation

Place the nuts or seeds into the Tall Cup. Screw the Nutribullet Extractor Blade on to the top of the cup. Invert the cup, press it down into the Nutribullet Power Base and twist it into place. Blast them for 30 seconds. Put the rest of the solid ingredients into the cup and press them down below the Max Line. Add the fluid base to fill the cup up to the Max Line. Screw the Nutribullet Extractor Blade on to the top of the cup. Invert the cup, press it down into the Nutribullet Power Base and twist it into place. Blast the mixture until it is really smooth (20 or so seconds). **Enjoy!**

Mint Mirage

Ingredients

1 Cup/Handful of Mint (40 grams or 1½ oz)
1 Cup/Handful of Bok Choy (40 grams or 1½ oz)
½ Cup of Blackberries (60 grams or 2 oz)
1 Cup/Handful of sliced Tomato (120 grams or 4 oz)
30 grams or 1 oz of Almonds
150 ml / 5 fl oz of Almond Milk (Unsweetened)

Protein 11g, Fat 18g, Carb 9g, Fibre 11g, 266 Kcals

Preparation

Place the nuts or seeds into the Tall Cup. Screw the Nutribullet Extractor Blade on to the top of the cup. Invert the cup, press it down into the Nutribullet Power Base and twist it into place. Blast them for 30 seconds. Put the rest of the solid ingredients into the cup and press them down below the Max Line. Add the fluid base to fill the cup up to the Max Line. Screw the Nutribullet Extractor Blade on to the top of the cup. Invert the cup, press it down into the Nutribullet Power Base and twist it into place. Blast the mixture until it is really smooth (20 or so seconds). **Enjoy!**

Blackberry joins Tomato

Ingredients

2 Cups/Handfuls of Spinach (80 grams or 3 oz)
½ Cup of Blackberries (60 grams or 2 oz)
1 Cup/Handful of sliced Tomato (120 grams or 4 oz)
30 grams or 1 oz of Hazelnuts
150 ml / 5 fl oz of Almond Milk (Unsweetened)

Protein 9g, Fat 21g, Carb 9g, Fibre 10g, 273 Kcals

Preparation

Place the nuts or seeds into the Tall Cup. Screw the Nutribullet Extractor Blade on to the top of the cup. Invert the cup, press it down into the Nutribullet Power Base and twist it into place. Blast them for 30 seconds. Put the rest of the solid ingredients into the cup and press them down below the Max Line. Add the fluid base to fill the cup up to the Max Line. Screw the Nutribullet Extractor Blade on to the top of the cup. Invert the cup, press it down into the Nutribullet Power Base and twist it into place. Blast the mixture until it is really smooth (20 or so seconds). **Enjoy!**

Watercress in Pumpkin

Ingredients

1 Cup/Handful of Rocket/Arugura Lettuce (40 grams or 1½ oz)
1 Cup/Handful of Watercress (40 grams or 1½ oz)
½ Cup of Strawberries (60 grams or 2 oz)
1 Cup/Handful of sliced Tomato (120 grams or 4 oz)
22 grams or ¾ oz of Pumpkin Seeds
150 ml / 5 fl oz of Almond Milk (Unsweetened)

Protein 9g, Fat 12g, Carb 10g, Fibre 5g, 194 Kcals

Preparation

Place the nuts or seeds into the Tall Cup. Screw the Nutribullet Extractor Blade on to the top of the cup. Invert the cup, press it down into the Nutribullet Power Base and twist it into place. Blast them for 30 seconds. Put the rest of the solid ingredients into the cup and press them down below the Max Line. Add the fluid base to fill the cup up to the Max Line. Screw the Nutribullet Extractor Blade on to the top of the cup. Invert the cup, press it down into the Nutribullet Power Base and twist it into place. Blast the mixture until it is really smooth (20 or so seconds). **Enjoy!**

Hazelnut Healer

Ingredients

1 Cup/Handful of Mint (40 grams or 1½ oz)
1 Cup/Handful of Spinach (40 grams or 1½ oz)
½ Cup of Strawberries (60 grams or 2 oz)
1 Cup/Handful of sliced Tomato (120 grams or 4 oz)
30 grams or 1 oz of Hazelnuts
150 ml / 5 fl oz of Almond Milk (Unsweetened)

Protein 9g, Fat 21g, Carb 10g, Fibre 10g, 275 Kcals

Preparation

Place the nuts or seeds into the Tall Cup. Screw the Nutribullet Extractor Blade on to the top of the cup. Invert the cup, press it down into the Nutribullet Power Base and twist it into place. Blast them for 30 seconds. Put the rest of the solid ingredients into the cup and press them down below the Max Line. Add the fluid base to fill the cup up to the Max Line. Screw the Nutribullet Extractor Blade on to the top of the cup. Invert the cup, press it down into the Nutribullet Power Base and twist it into place. Blast the mixture until it is really smooth (20 or so seconds). **Enjoy!**

Strawberry on Tomato

Ingredients

2 Cups/Handfuls of Mint (80 grams or 3 oz)
½ Cup of Strawberries (60 grams or 2 oz)
1 Cup/Handful of sliced Tomato (120 grams or 4 oz)
30 grams or 1 oz of Hazelnuts
150 ml / 5 fl oz of Almond Milk (Unsweetened)

Protein 9g, Fat 21g, Carb 10g, Fibre 12g, 283 Kcals

Preparation

Place the nuts or seeds into the Tall Cup. Screw the Nutribullet Extractor Blade on to the top of the cup. Invert the cup, press it down into the Nutribullet Power Base and twist it into place. Blast them for 30 seconds. Put the rest of the solid ingredients into the cup and press them down below the Max Line. Add the fluid base to fill the cup up to the Max Line. Screw the Nutribullet Extractor Blade on to the top of the cup. Invert the cup, press it down into the Nutribullet Power Base and twist it into place. Blast the mixture until it is really smooth (20 or so seconds). **Enjoy!**

Avocado Adventure

Ingredients

1 Cup/Handful of Spinach (40 grams or 1½ oz)
1 Cup/Handful of Bok Choy (40 grams or 1½ oz)
½ Cup of Avocado slices (60 grams or 2 oz)
1 Cup/Handful of sliced Tomato (120 grams or 4 oz)
22 grams or ¾ oz of Flax Seeds
150 ml / 5 fl oz of Hazelnut Milk

Protein 8g, Fat 21g, Carb 10g, Fibre 13g, 292 Kcals

Preparation

Place the nuts or seeds into the Tall Cup. Screw the Nutribullet Extractor Blade on to the top of the cup. Invert the cup, press it down into the Nutribullet Power Base and twist it into place. Blast them for 30 seconds. Put the rest of the solid ingredients into the cup and press them down below the Max Line. Add the fluid base to fill the cup up to the Max Line. Screw the Nutribullet Extractor Blade on to the top of the cup. Invert the cup, press it down into the Nutribullet Power Base and twist it into place. Blast the mixture until it is really smooth (20 or so seconds). *Enjoy!*

Green Cabbage needs Pecan

Ingredients

2 Cups/Handfuls of Green Cabbage (80 grams or 3 oz)
½ Cup of Strawberries (60 grams or 2 oz)
1 Cup/Handful of sliced Tomato (120 grams or 4 oz)
30 grams or 1 oz of Pecans
150 ml / 5 fl oz of Almond Milk (Unsweetened)

Protein 6g, Fat 24g, Carb 11g, Fibre 8g, 287 Kcals

Preparation

Place the nuts or seeds into the Tall Cup. Screw the Nutribullet Extractor Blade on to the top of the cup. Invert the cup, press it down into the Nutribullet Power Base and twist it into place. Blast them for 30 seconds. Put the rest of the solid ingredients into the cup and press them down below the Max Line. Add the fluid base to fill the cup up to the Max Line. Screw the Nutribullet Extractor Blade on to the top of the cup. Invert the cup, press it down into the Nutribullet Power Base and twist it into place. Blast the mixture until it is really smooth (20 or so seconds). *Enjoy!*

Watercress and Flax Machine

Ingredients

2 Cups/Handfuls of Watercress (80 grams or 3 oz)
½ Cup of Blackberries (60 grams or 2 oz)
1 Cup/Handful of sliced Tomato (120 grams or 4 oz)
22 grams or ¾ oz of Flax Seeds
150 ml / 5 fl oz of Coconut Milk

Protein 8g, Fat 11g, Carb 11g, Fibre 11g, 203 Kcals

Preparation

Place the nuts or seeds into the Tall Cup. Screw the Nutribullet Extractor Blade on to the top of the cup. Invert the cup, press it down into the Nutribullet Power Base and twist it into place. Blast them for 30 seconds. Put the rest of the solid ingredients into the cup and press them down below the Max Line. Add the fluid base to fill the cup up to the Max Line. Screw the Nutribullet Extractor Blade on to the top of the cup. Invert the cup, press it down into the Nutribullet Power Base and twist it into place. Blast the mixture until it is really smooth (20 or so seconds). **Enjoy!**

Radiant Skin Nourishing Blasts
High in Anti oxidants, Caroteinoids, Polyphenols, Pectin, Zinc, Vitamins A, C

Avocado and Sesame Avarice

Ingredients

1 Cup/Handful of Rocket/Arugura Lettuce (40 grams or 1½ oz)
1 Cup/Handful of Watercress (40 grams or 1½ oz)
1 Cup/Handful of Avocado slices (120 grams or 4 oz)
22 grams or ¾ oz of Sesame Seeds Hulled
75 ml / 2½ fl oz of Almond Milk (Unsweetened)
75 ml / 2½ fl oz of Greek Yoghurt

Protein 11g, Fat 38g, Carb 8g, Fibre 11g, 437 Kcals

Preparation

Place the nuts or seeds into the Tall Cup. Screw the Nutribullet Extractor Blade on to the top of the cup. Invert the cup, press it down into the Nutribullet Power Base and twist it into place. Blast them for 30 seconds. Put the rest of the solid ingredients into the cup and press them down below the Max Line. Add the fluid base to fill the cup up to the Max Line. Screw the Nutribullet Extractor Blade on to the top of the cup. Invert the cup, press it down into the Nutribullet Power Base and twist it into place. Blast the mixture until it is really smooth (20 or so seconds). **Enjoy!**

Bok Choy goes Mint

Ingredients

1 Cup/Handful of Bok Choy (40 grams or 1½ oz)
1 Cup/Handful of Mint (40 grams or 1½ oz)
1 Cup/Handful of Avocado slices (120 grams or 4 oz)
30 grams or 1 oz of Pecans
75 ml / 2½ fl oz of Almond Milk (Unsweetened)
75 ml / 2½ fl oz of Greek Yoghurt

Protein 11g, Fat 48g, Carb 9g, Fibre 14g, 525 Kcals

Preparation

Place the nuts or seeds into the Tall Cup. Screw the Nutribullet Extractor Blade on to the top of the cup. Invert the cup, press it down into the Nutribullet Power Base and twist it into place. Blast them for 30 seconds. Put the rest of the solid ingredients into the cup and press them down below the Max Line. Add the fluid base to fill the cup up to the Max Line. Screw the Nutribullet Extractor Blade on to the top of the cup. Invert the cup, press it down into the Nutribullet Power Base and twist it into place. Blast the mixture until it is really smooth (20 or so seconds). **Enjoy!**

Green Cabbage and Avocado Adventure

Ingredients

1 Cup/Handful of Green Cabbage (40 grams or 1½ oz)
1 Cup/Handful of Bok Choy (40 grams or 1½ oz)
1 Cup/Handful of Avocado slices (120 grams or 4 oz)
30 grams or 1 oz of Pecans
75 ml / 2½ fl oz of Almond Milk (Unsweetened)
75 ml / 2½ fl oz of Greek Yoghurt

Protein 10g, Fat 47g, Carb 9g, Fibre 13g, 518 Kcals

Preparation

Place the nuts or seeds into the Tall Cup. Screw the Nutribullet Extractor Blade on to the top of the cup. Invert the cup, press it down into the Nutribullet Power Base and twist it into place. Blast them for 30 seconds. Put the rest of the solid ingredients into the cup and press them down below the Max Line. Add the fluid base to fill the cup up to the Max Line. Screw the Nutribullet Extractor Blade on to the top of the cup. Invert the cup, press it down into the Nutribullet Power Base and twist it into place. Blast the mixture until it is really smooth (20 or so seconds). **Enjoy!**

Spinach embraces Avocado

Ingredients

1 Cup/Handful of Black Kale de-stemmed (40 grams or 1½ oz)
1 Cup/Handful of Spinach (40 grams or 1½ oz)
½ Cup of Avocado slices (60 grams or 2 oz)
½ Cup of Strawberries (60 grams or 2 oz)
22 grams or ¾ oz of Sesame Seeds Hulled
75 ml / 2½ fl oz of Almond Milk (Unsweetened)
75 ml / 2½ fl oz of Greek Yoghurt

Protein 12g, Fat 30g, Carb 10g, Fibre 9g, 373 Kcals

Preparation

Place the nuts or seeds into the Tall Cup. Screw the Nutribullet Extractor Blade on to the top of the cup. Invert the cup, press it down into the Nutribullet Power Base and twist it into place. Blast them for 30 seconds. Put the rest of the solid ingredients into the cup and press them down below the Max Line. Add the fluid base to fill the cup up to the Max Line. Screw the Nutribullet Extractor Blade on to the top of the cup. Invert the cup, press it down into the Nutribullet Power Base and twist it into place. Blast the mixture until it is really smooth (20 or so seconds). *Enjoy!*

Sesame Session

Ingredients

1 Cup/Handful of Watercress (40 grams or 1½ oz)
1 Cup/Handful of Bok Choy (40 grams or 1½ oz)
1 Cup/Handful of Blackberries (120 grams or 4 oz)
22 grams or ¾ oz of Sesame Seeds Hulled
75 ml / 2½ fl oz of Almond Milk (Unsweetened)
75 ml / 2½ fl oz of Greek Yoghurt

Protein 11g, Fat 21g, Carb 10g, Fibre 9g, 296 Kcals

Preparation

Place the nuts or seeds into the Tall Cup. Screw the Nutribullet Extractor Blade on to the top of the cup. Invert the cup, press it down into the Nutribullet Power Base and twist it into place. Blast them for 30 seconds. Put the rest of the solid ingredients into the cup and press them down below the Max Line. Add the fluid base to fill the cup up to the Max Line. Screw the Nutribullet Extractor Blade on to the top of the cup. Invert the cup, press it down into the Nutribullet Power Base and twist it into place. Blast the mixture until it is really smooth (20 or so seconds). *Enjoy!*

Green Cabbage loves Pumpkin

Ingredients

1 Cup/Handful of Spinach (40 grams or 1½ oz)
1 Cup/Handful of Green Cabbage (40 grams or 1½ oz)
1 Cup/Handful of Avocado slices (120 grams or 4 oz)
22 grams or ¾ oz of Pumpkin Seeds
75 ml / 2½ fl oz of Almond Milk (Unsweetened)
75 ml / 2½ fl oz of Greek Yoghurt

Protein 13g, Fat 35g, Carb 10g, Fibre 11g, 439 Kcals

Preparation

Place the nuts or seeds into the Tall Cup. Screw the Nutribullet Extractor Blade on to the top of the cup. Invert the cup, press it down into the Nutribullet Power Base and twist it into place. Blast them for 30 seconds. Put the rest of the solid ingredients into the cup and press them down below the Max Line. Add the fluid base to fill the cup up to the Max Line. Screw the Nutribullet Extractor Blade on to the top of the cup. Invert the cup, press it down into the Nutribullet Power Base and twist it into place. Blast the mixture until it is really smooth (20 or so seconds). **Enjoy!**

Mint meets Avocado

Ingredients

1 Cup/Handful of Green Cabbage (40 grams or 1½ oz)
1 Cup/Handful of Mint (40 grams or 1½ oz)
1 Cup/Handful of Avocado slices (120 grams or 4 oz)
22 grams or ¾ oz of Pumpkin Seeds
75 ml / 2½ fl oz of Almond Milk (Unsweetened)
75 ml / 2½ fl oz of Greek Yoghurt

Protein 13g, Fat 36g, Carb 10g, Fibre 13g, 447 Kcals

Preparation

Place the nuts or seeds into the Tall Cup. Screw the Nutribullet Extractor Blade on to the top of the cup. Invert the cup, press it down into the Nutribullet Power Base and twist it into place. Blast them for 30 seconds. Put the rest of the solid ingredients into the cup and press them down below the Max Line. Add the fluid base to fill the cup up to the Max Line. Screw the Nutribullet Extractor Blade on to the top of the cup. Invert the cup, press it down into the Nutribullet Power Base and twist it into place. Blast the mixture until it is really smooth (20 or so seconds). **Enjoy!**

Bok Choy meets Sesame

Ingredients

1 Cup/Handful of Black Kale de-stemmed (40 grams or 1½ oz)
1 Cup/Handful of Bok Choy (40 grams or 1½ oz)
1 Cup/Handful of Avocado slices (120 grams or 4 oz)
22 grams or ¾ oz of Sesame Seeds Hulled
150 ml / 5 fl oz of Dairy Milk Semi Skimmed

Protein 14g, Fat 34g, Carb 11g, Fibre 11g, 417 Kcals

Preparation

Place the nuts or seeds into the Tall Cup. Screw the Nutribullet Extractor Blade on to the top of the cup. Invert the cup, press it down into the Nutribullet Power Base and twist it into place. Blast them for 30 seconds. Put the rest of the solid ingredients into the cup and press them down below the Max Line. Add the fluid base to fill the cup up to the Max Line. Screw the Nutribullet Extractor Blade on to the top of the cup. Invert the cup, press it down into the Nutribullet Power Base and twist it into place. Blast the mixture until it is really smooth (20 or so seconds). **Enjoy!**

Watercress and Sesame Garden

Ingredients

2 Cups/Handfuls of Watercress (80 grams or 3 oz)
½ Cup of Blackberries (60 grams or 2 oz)
½ Cup of Raspberries (60 grams or 2 oz)
22 grams or ¾ oz of Sesame Seeds Hulled
75 ml / 2½ fl oz of Almond Milk (Unsweetened)
75 ml / 2½ fl oz of Greek Yoghurt

Protein 11g, Fat 21g, Carb 11g, Fibre 10g, 300 Kcals

Preparation

Place the nuts or seeds into the Tall Cup. Screw the Nutribullet Extractor Blade on to the top of the cup. Invert the cup, press it down into the Nutribullet Power Base and twist it into place. Blast them for 30 seconds. Put the rest of the solid ingredients into the cup and press them down below the Max Line. Add the fluid base to fill the cup up to the Max Line. Screw the Nutribullet Extractor Blade on to the top of the cup. Invert the cup, press it down into the Nutribullet Power Base and twist it into place. Blast the mixture until it is really smooth (20 or so seconds). **Enjoy!**

Black Kale in Avocado

Ingredients

1 Cup/Handful of Rocket/Arugura Lettuce (40 grams or 1½ oz)
1 Cup/Handful of Black Kale de-stemmed (40 grams or 1½ oz)
1 Cup/Handful of Avocado slices (120 grams or 4 oz)
30 grams or 1 oz of Pecans
75 ml / 2½ fl oz of Coconut Milk
75 ml / 2½ fl oz of Greek Yoghurt

Protein 10g, Fat 48g, Carb 11g, Fibre 12g, 528 Kcals

Preparation

Place the nuts or seeds into the Tall Cup. Screw the Nutribullet Extractor Blade on to the top of the cup. Invert the cup, press it down into the Nutribullet Power Base and twist it into place. Blast them for 30 seconds. Put the rest of the solid ingredients into the cup and press them down below the Max Line. Add the fluid base to fill the cup up to the Max Line. Screw the Nutribullet Extractor Blade on to the top of the cup. Invert the cup, press it down into the Nutribullet Power Base and twist it into place. Blast the mixture until it is really smooth (20 or so seconds). **Enjoy!**

Ultra Low Carb Double Fruit Blasts
Carbs are the poison exercise is the antidote (With Carb Grams)

Bok Choy and Avocado Fix

Ingredients

1 Cup/Handful of Watercress (40 grams or 1½ oz)
1 Cup/Handful of Bok Choy (40 grams or 1½ oz)
1 Cup/Handful of Avocado slices (120 grams or 4 oz)
22 grams or ¾ oz of Flax Seeds
75 ml / 2½ fl oz of Almond Milk (Unsweetened)
75 ml / 2½ fl oz of Greek Yoghurt

Protein 11g, Fat 35g, Carb 8g, Fibre 15g, 422 Kcals

Preparation

Place the nuts or seeds into the Tall Cup. Screw the Nutribullet Extractor Blade on to the top of the cup. Invert the cup, press it down into the Nutribullet Power Base and twist it into place. Blast them for 30 seconds. Put the rest of the solid ingredients into the cup and press them down below the Max Line. Add the fluid base to fill the cup up to the Max Line. Screw the Nutribullet Extractor Blade on to the top of the cup. Invert the cup, press it down into the Nutribullet Power Base and twist it into place. Blast the mixture until it is really smooth (20 or so seconds). **Enjoy!**

Lettuce and Flax Bliss

Ingredients

1 Cup/Handful of Lettuce Leaves (40 grams or 1½ oz)
1 Cup/Handful of Black Kale de-stemmed (40 grams or 1½ oz)
1 Cup/Handful of Avocado slices (120 grams or 4 oz)
22 grams or ¾ oz of Flax Seeds
150 ml / 5 fl oz of Coconut Milk

Protein 8g, Fat 29g, Carb 8g, Fibre 16g, 360 Kcals

Preparation

Place the nuts or seeds into the Tall Cup. Screw the Nutribullet Extractor Blade on to the top of the cup. Invert the cup, press it down into the Nutribullet Power Base and twist it into place. Blast them for 30 seconds. Put the rest of the solid ingredients into the cup and press them down below the Max Line. Add the fluid base to fill the cup up to the Max Line. Screw the Nutribullet Extractor Blade on to the top of the cup. Invert the cup, press it down into the Nutribullet Power Base and twist it into place. Blast the mixture until it is really smooth (20 or so seconds). ***Enjoy!***

Lettuce and Hazelnut Energizer

Ingredients

1 Cup/Handful of Rocket/Arugura Lettuce (40 grams or 1½ oz)
1 Cup/Handful of Lettuce Leaves (40 grams or 1½ oz)
½ Cup of Avocado slices (60 grams or 2 oz)
½ Cup of Strawberries (60 grams or 2 oz)
30 grams or 1 oz of Hazelnuts
150 ml / 5 fl oz of Almond Milk (Unsweetened)

Protein 8g, Fat 29g, Carb 8g, Fibre 10g, 335 Kcals

Preparation

Place the nuts or seeds into the Tall Cup. Screw the Nutribullet Extractor Blade on to the top of the cup. Invert the cup, press it down into the Nutribullet Power Base and twist it into place. Blast them for 30 seconds. Put the rest of the solid ingredients into the cup and press them down below the Max Line. Add the fluid base to fill the cup up to the Max Line. Screw the Nutribullet Extractor Blade on to the top of the cup. Invert the cup, press it down into the Nutribullet Power Base and twist it into place. Blast the mixture until it is really smooth (20 or so seconds). ***Enjoy!***

Spinach and Flax Consortium

Ingredients

1 Cup/Handful of Spinach (40 grams or 1½ oz)
1 Cup/Handful of Black Kale de-stemmed (40 grams or 1½ oz)
1 Cup/Handful of Avocado slices (120 grams or 4 oz)
22 grams or ¾ oz of Flax Seeds
75 ml / 2½ fl oz of Almond Milk (Unsweetened)
75 ml / 2½ fl oz of Greek Yoghurt

Protein 12g, Fat 36g, Carb 8g, Fibre 16g, 436 Kcals

Preparation

Place the nuts or seeds into the Tall Cup. Screw the Nutribullet Extractor Blade on to the top of the cup. Invert the cup, press it down into the Nutribullet Power Base and twist it into place. Blast them for 30 seconds. Put the rest of the solid ingredients into the cup and press them down below the Max Line. Add the fluid base to fill the cup up to the Max Line. Screw the Nutribullet Extractor Blade on to the top of the cup. Invert the cup, press it down into the Nutribullet Power Base and twist it into place. Blast the mixture until it is really smooth (20 or so seconds). **Enjoy!**

Walnut Wonder

Ingredients

1 Cup/Handful of Watercress (40 grams or 1½ oz)
1 Cup/Handful of Mint (40 grams or 1½ oz)
1 Cup/Handful of Blackberries (120 grams or 4 oz)
30 grams or 1 oz of Walnuts
150 ml / 5 fl oz of Almond Milk (Unsweetened)

Protein 9g, Fat 22g, Carb 8g, Fibre 12g, 289 Kcals

Preparation

Place the nuts or seeds into the Tall Cup. Screw the Nutribullet Extractor Blade on to the top of the cup. Invert the cup, press it down into the Nutribullet Power Base and twist it into place. Blast them for 30 seconds. Put the rest of the solid ingredients into the cup and press them down below the Max Line. Add the fluid base to fill the cup up to the Max Line. Screw the Nutribullet Extractor Blade on to the top of the cup. Invert the cup, press it down into the Nutribullet Power Base and twist it into place. Blast the mixture until it is really smooth (20 or so seconds). **Enjoy!**

Apricot and Flax Orchestra

Ingredients

2 Cups/Handfuls of Black Kale de-stemmed (80 grams or 3 oz)
½ Cup of Apricot halves (60 grams or 2 oz)
½ Cup of Avocado slices (60 grams or 2 oz)
22 grams or ¾ oz of Flax Seeds
150 ml / 5 fl oz of Almond Milk (Unsweetened)

Protein 9g, Fat 21g, Carb 8g, Fibre 14g, 289 Kcals

Preparation

Place the nuts or seeds into the Tall Cup. Screw the Nutribullet Extractor Blade on to the top of the cup. Invert the cup, press it down into the Nutribullet Power Base and twist it into place. Blast them for 30 seconds. Put the rest of the solid ingredients into the cup and press them down below the Max Line. Add the fluid base to fill the cup up to the Max Line. Screw the Nutribullet Extractor Blade on to the top of the cup. Invert the cup, press it down into the Nutribullet Power Base and twist it into place. Blast the mixture until it is really smooth (20 or so seconds). **Enjoy!**

Watercress on Raspberry

Ingredients

2 Cups/Handfuls of Watercress (80 grams or 3 oz)
1 Cup/Handful of Raspberries (120 grams or 4 oz)
30 grams or 1 oz of Brazil nuts
150 ml / 5 fl oz of Almond Milk (Unsweetened)

Protein 8g, Fat 23g, Carb 9g, Fibre 11g, 288 Kcals

Preparation

Place the nuts or seeds into the Tall Cup. Screw the Nutribullet Extractor Blade on to the top of the cup. Invert the cup, press it down into the Nutribullet Power Base and twist it into place. Blast them for 30 seconds. Put the rest of the solid ingredients into the cup and press them down below the Max Line. Add the fluid base to fill the cup up to the Max Line. Screw the Nutribullet Extractor Blade on to the top of the cup. Invert the cup, press it down into the Nutribullet Power Base and twist it into place. Blast the mixture until it is really smooth (20 or so seconds). **Enjoy!**

Cranberry Cocktail

Ingredients

1 Cup/Handful of Mint (40 grams or 1½ oz)
1 Cup/Handful of Lettuce Leaves (40 grams or 1½ oz)
½ Cup of Blackberries (60 grams or 2 oz)
½ Cup of Cranberries (60 grams or 2 oz)
22 grams or ¾ oz of Flax Seeds
150 ml / 5 fl oz of Almond Milk (Unsweetened)

Protein 7g, Fat 12g, Carb 9g, Fibre 16g, 214 Kcals

Preparation

Place the nuts or seeds into the Tall Cup. Screw the Nutribullet Extractor Blade on to the top of the cup. Invert the cup, press it down into the Nutribullet Power Base and twist it into place. Blast them for 30 seconds. Put the rest of the solid ingredients into the cup and press them down below the Max Line. Add the fluid base to fill the cup up to the Max Line. Screw the Nutribullet Extractor Blade on to the top of the cup. Invert the cup, press it down into the Nutribullet Power Base and twist it into place. Blast the mixture until it is really smooth (20 or so seconds). ***Enjoy!***

Cranberry and Walnut Blockbuster

Ingredients

2 Cups/Handfuls of Bok Choy (80 grams or 3 oz)
½ Cup of Cranberries (60 grams or 2 oz)
½ Cup of Avocado slices (60 grams or 2 oz)
30 grams or 1 oz of Walnuts
150 ml / 5 fl oz of Almond Milk (Unsweetened)

Protein 8g, Fat 30g, Carb 9g, Fibre 10g, 349 Kcals

Preparation

Place the nuts or seeds into the Tall Cup. Screw the Nutribullet Extractor Blade on to the top of the cup. Invert the cup, press it down into the Nutribullet Power Base and twist it into place. Blast them for 30 seconds. Put the rest of the solid ingredients into the cup and press them down below the Max Line. Add the fluid base to fill the cup up to the Max Line. Screw the Nutribullet Extractor Blade on to the top of the cup. Invert the cup, press it down into the Nutribullet Power Base and twist it into place. Blast the mixture until it is really smooth (20 or so seconds). ***Enjoy!***

Brazil Blend

Ingredients

1 Cup/Handful of Fennel (40 grams or 1½ oz)
1 Cup/Handful of Green Cabbage (40 grams or 1½ oz)
½ Cup of Avocado slices (60 grams or 2 oz)
½ Cup of Strawberries (60 grams or 2 oz)
30 grams or 1 oz of Brazil nuts
150 ml / 5 fl oz of Almond Milk (Unsweetened)

Protein 8g, Fat 31g, Carb 9g, Fibre 10g, 354 Kcals

Preparation

Place the nuts or seeds into the Tall Cup. Screw the Nutribullet Extractor Blade on to the top of the cup. Invert the cup, press it down into the Nutribullet Power Base and twist it into place. Blast them for 30 seconds. Put the rest of the solid ingredients into the cup and press them down below the Max Line. Add the fluid base to fill the cup up to the Max Line. Screw the Nutribullet Extractor Blade on to the top of the cup. Invert the cup, press it down into the Nutribullet Power Base and twist it into place. Blast the mixture until it is really smooth (20 or so seconds). **Enjoy!**

Verdant Tonic

Ingredients

2 Cups/Handfuls of Black Kale de-stemmed (80 grams or 3 oz)
1 Cup/Handful of Avocado slices (120 grams or 4 oz)
30 grams or 1 oz of Brazil nuts
75 ml / 2½ fl oz of Almond Milk (Unsweetened)
75 ml / 2½ fl oz of Greek Yoghurt

Protein 13g, Fat 47g, Carb 9g, Fibre 13g, 521 Kcals

Preparation

Place the nuts or seeds into the Tall Cup. Screw the Nutribullet Extractor Blade on to the top of the cup. Invert the cup, press it down into the Nutribullet Power Base and twist it into place. Blast them for 30 seconds. Put the rest of the solid ingredients into the cup and press them down below the Max Line. Add the fluid base to fill the cup up to the Max Line. Screw the Nutribullet Extractor Blade on to the top of the cup. Invert the cup, press it down into the Nutribullet Power Base and twist it into place. Blast the mixture until it is really smooth (20 or so seconds). **Enjoy!**

Rocket Rocker

Ingredients

1 Cup/Handful of Rocket/Arugura Lettuce (40 grams or 1½ oz)
1 Cup/Handful of Spinach (40 grams or 1½ oz)
½ Cup of Strawberries (60 grams or 2 oz)
½ Cup of Grapefruit segments (60 grams or 2 oz)
22 grams or ¾ oz of Flax Seeds
150 ml / 5 fl oz of Almond Milk (Unsweetened)

Protein 7g, Fat 11g, Carb 9g, Fibre 10g, 190 Kcals

Preparation

Place the nuts or seeds into the Tall Cup. Screw the Nutribullet Extractor Blade on to the top of the cup. Invert the cup, press it down into the Nutribullet Power Base and twist it into place. Blast them for 30 seconds. Put the rest of the solid ingredients into the cup and press them down below the Max Line. Add the fluid base to fill the cup up to the Max Line. Screw the Nutribullet Extractor Blade on to the top of the cup. Invert the cup, press it down into the Nutribullet Power Base and twist it into place. Blast the mixture until it is really smooth (20 or so seconds). **Enjoy!**

Lettuce and Pecan Sensation

Ingredients

1 Cup/Handful of Watercress (40 grams or 1½ oz)
1 Cup/Handful of Lettuce Leaves (40 grams or 1½ oz)
½ Cup of Avocado slices (60 grams or 2 oz)
½ Cup of Clementine slices (60 grams or 2 oz)
30 grams or 1 oz of Pecans
150 ml / 5 fl oz of Almond Milk (Unsweetened)

Protein 6g, Fat 32g, Carb 9g, Fibre 10g, 362 Kcals

Preparation

Place the nuts or seeds into the Tall Cup. Screw the Nutribullet Extractor Blade on to the top of the cup. Invert the cup, press it down into the Nutribullet Power Base and twist it into place. Blast them for 30 seconds. Put the rest of the solid ingredients into the cup and press them down below the Max Line. Add the fluid base to fill the cup up to the Max Line. Screw the Nutribullet Extractor Blade on to the top of the cup. Invert the cup, press it down into the Nutribullet Power Base and twist it into place. Blast the mixture until it is really smooth (20 or so seconds). **Enjoy!**

Watercress and Pecan Medley

Ingredients

1 Cup/Handful of Green Cabbage (40 grams or 1½ oz)
1 Cup/Handful of Watercress (40 grams or 1½ oz)
1 Cup/Handful of Avocado slices (120 grams or 4 oz)
30 grams or 1 oz of Pecans
150 ml / 5 fl oz of Hazelnut Milk

Protein 7g, Fat 42g, Carb 10g, Fibre 13g, 457 Kcals

Preparation

Place the nuts or seeds into the Tall Cup. Screw the Nutribullet Extractor Blade on to the top of the cup. Invert the cup, press it down into the Nutribullet Power Base and twist it into place. Blast them for 30 seconds. Put the rest of the solid ingredients into the cup and press them down below the Max Line. Add the fluid base to fill the cup up to the Max Line. Screw the Nutribullet Extractor Blade on to the top of the cup. Invert the cup, press it down into the Nutribullet Power Base and twist it into place. Blast the mixture until it is really smooth (20 or so seconds). **Enjoy!**

Avocado goes Hazelnut

Ingredients

2 Cups/Handfuls of Rocket/Arugura Lettuce (80 grams or 3 oz)
1 Cup/Handful of Avocado slices (120 grams or 4 oz)
30 grams or 1 oz of Hazelnuts
75 ml / 2½ fl oz of Almond Milk (Unsweetened)
75 ml / 2½ fl oz of Greek Yoghurt

Protein 11g, Fat 44g, Carb 10g, Fibre 12g, 495 Kcals

Preparation

Place the nuts or seeds into the Tall Cup. Screw the Nutribullet Extractor Blade on to the top of the cup. Invert the cup, press it down into the Nutribullet Power Base and twist it into place. Blast them for 30 seconds. Put the rest of the solid ingredients into the cup and press them down below the Max Line. Add the fluid base to fill the cup up to the Max Line. Screw the Nutribullet Extractor Blade on to the top of the cup. Invert the cup, press it down into the Nutribullet Power Base and twist it into place. Blast the mixture until it is really smooth (20 or so seconds). **Enjoy!**

Lettuce joins Nectarine

Ingredients

1 Cup/Handful of Lettuce Leaves (40 grams or 1½ oz)
1 Cup/Handful of Bok Choy (40 grams or 1½ oz)
½ Cup of Nectarine segments (60 grams or 2 oz)
½ Cup of Raspberries (60 grams or 2 oz)
22 grams or ¾ oz of Sesame Seeds Hulled
150 ml / 5 fl oz of Almond Milk (Unsweetened)

Protein 7g, Fat 15g, Carb 10g, Fibre 8g, 220 Kcals

Preparation

Place the nuts or seeds into the Tall Cup. Screw the Nutribullet Extractor Blade on to the top of the cup. Invert the cup, press it down into the Nutribullet Power Base and twist it into place. Blast them for 30 seconds. Put the rest of the solid ingredients into the cup and press them down below the Max Line. Add the fluid base to fill the cup up to the Max Line. Screw the Nutribullet Extractor Blade on to the top of the cup. Invert the cup, press it down into the Nutribullet Power Base and twist it into place. Blast the mixture until it is really smooth (20 or so seconds). ***Enjoy!***

Green Cabbage and Blackberry Supermodel

Ingredients

1 Cup/Handful of Rocket/Arugura Lettuce (40 grams or 1½ oz)
1 Cup/Handful of Green Cabbage (40 grams or 1½ oz)
½ Cup of Blackberries (60 grams or 2 oz)
½ Cup of Avocado slices (60 grams or 2 oz)
22 grams or ¾ oz of Sesame Seeds Hulled
150 ml / 5 fl oz of Coconut Milk

Protein 7g, Fat 23g, Carb 10g, Fibre 10g, 299 Kcals

Preparation

Place the nuts or seeds into the Tall Cup. Screw the Nutribullet Extractor Blade on to the top of the cup. Invert the cup, press it down into the Nutribullet Power Base and twist it into place. Blast them for 30 seconds. Put the rest of the solid ingredients into the cup and press them down below the Max Line. Add the fluid base to fill the cup up to the Max Line. Screw the Nutribullet Extractor Blade on to the top of the cup. Invert the cup, press it down into the Nutribullet Power Base and twist it into place. Blast the mixture until it is really smooth (20 or so seconds). ***Enjoy!***

Grapefruit and Brazil Guru

Ingredients

1 Cup/Handful of Spinach (40 grams or 1½ oz)
1 Cup/Handful of Lettuce Leaves (40 grams or 1½ oz)
½ Cup of Grapefruit segments (60 grams or 2 oz)
½ Cup of Raspberries (60 grams or 2 oz)
30 grams or 1 oz of Brazil nuts
150 ml / 5 fl oz of Almond Milk (Unsweetened)

Protein 8g, Fat 23g, Carb 10g, Fibre 9g, 283 Kcals

Preparation

Place the nuts or seeds into the Tall Cup. Screw the Nutribullet Extractor Blade on to the top of the cup. Invert the cup, press it down into the Nutribullet Power Base and twist it into place. Blast them for 30 seconds. Put the rest of the solid ingredients into the cup and press them down below the Max Line. Add the fluid base to fill the cup up to the Max Line. Screw the Nutribullet Extractor Blade on to the top of the cup. Invert the cup, press it down into the Nutribullet Power Base and twist it into place. Blast the mixture until it is really smooth (20 or so seconds). **Enjoy!**

Rocket and Avocado Gala

Ingredients

1 Cup/Handful of Rocket/Arugura Lettuce (40 grams or 1½ oz)
1 Cup/Handful of Spinach (40 grams or 1½ oz)
1 Cup/Handful of Avocado slices (120 grams or 4 oz)
22 grams or ¾ oz of Pumpkin Seeds
150 ml / 5 fl oz of Hazelnut Milk

Protein 10g, Fat 30g, Carb 10g, Fibre 11g, 375 Kcals

Preparation

Place the nuts or seeds into the Tall Cup. Screw the Nutribullet Extractor Blade on to the top of the cup. Invert the cup, press it down into the Nutribullet Power Base and twist it into place. Blast them for 30 seconds. Put the rest of the solid ingredients into the cup and press them down below the Max Line. Add the fluid base to fill the cup up to the Max Line. Screw the Nutribullet Extractor Blade on to the top of the cup. Invert the cup, press it down into the Nutribullet Power Base and twist it into place. Blast the mixture until it is really smooth (20 or so seconds). **Enjoy!**

Water Melon Waistline

Ingredients

1 Cup/Handful of Fennel (40 grams or 1½ oz)
1 Cup/Handful of Broccoli Florets (40 grams or 1½ oz)
½ Cup of Avocado slices (60 grams or 2 oz)
½ Cup of Water Melon chunks (60 grams or 2 oz)
30 grams or 1 oz of Brazil nuts
150 ml / 5 fl oz of Almond Milk (Unsweetened)

Protein 8g, Fat 31g, Carb 10g, Fibre 9g, 357 Kcals

Preparation

Place the nuts or seeds into the Tall Cup. Screw the Nutribullet Extractor Blade on to the top of the cup. Invert the cup, press it down into the Nutribullet Power Base and twist it into place. Blast them for 30 seconds. Put the rest of the solid ingredients into the cup and press them down below the Max Line. Add the fluid base to fill the cup up to the Max Line. Screw the Nutribullet Extractor Blade on to the top of the cup. Invert the cup, press it down into the Nutribullet Power Base and twist it into place. Blast the mixture until it is really smooth (20 or so seconds). **Enjoy!**

Ultra Low Carb Double Fruit Smoothies
Carbs are the poison exercise is the antidote (With Carb Grams)

Verdant Therapy

Ingredients

1 Cup/Handful of Black Kale de-stemmed (40 grams or 1½ oz)
1 Cup/Handful of Green Cabbage (40 grams or 1½ oz)
1 Cup/Handful of Avocado slices (120 grams or 4 oz)
150 ml / 5 fl oz of Almond Milk (Unsweetened)

Protein 5g, Fat 20g, Carb 4g, Fibre 11g, 235 Kcals

Preparation

Put all the solid ingredients into the Tall Cup and press them down below the Max Line. Add the fluid base to fill the cup up to the Max Line. Screw the Nutribullet Extractor Blade on to the top of the cup. Invert the cup, press it down into the Nutribullet Power Base and twist it into place. Blast the mixture until it is really smooth (20 or so seconds). **Enjoy!**

Spinach loves Green Cabbage

Ingredients

1 Cup/Handful of Spinach (40 grams or 1½ oz)
1 Cup/Handful of Green Cabbage (40 grams or 1½ oz)
1 Cup/Handful of Blackberries (120 grams or 4 oz)
150 ml / 5 fl oz of Almond Milk (Unsweetened)

Protein 4g, Fat 2g, Carb 7g, Fibre 9g, 90 Kcals

Preparation

Put all the solid ingredients into the Tall Cup and press them down below the Max Line. Add the fluid base to fill the cup up to the Max Line. Screw the Nutribullet Extractor Blade on to the top of the cup. Invert the cup, press it down into the Nutribullet Power Base and twist it into place. Blast the mixture until it is really smooth (20 or so seconds). **Enjoy!**

Watercress embraces Bok Choy

Ingredients

1 Cup/Handful of Watercress (40 grams or 1½ oz)
1 Cup/Handful of Bok Choy (40 grams or 1½ oz)
1 Cup/Handful of Strawberries (120 grams or 4 oz)
150 ml / 5 fl oz of Almond Milk (Unsweetened)

Protein 3g, Fat 2g, Carb 8g, Fibre 4g, 67 Kcals

Preparation

Put all the solid ingredients into the Tall Cup and press them down below the Max Line. Add the fluid base to fill the cup up to the Max Line. Screw the Nutribullet Extractor Blade on to the top of the cup. Invert the cup, press it down into the Nutribullet Power Base and twist it into place. Blast the mixture until it is really smooth (20 or so seconds). **Enjoy!**

Mint and Lettuce Heaven

Ingredients

1 Cup/Handful of Mint (40 grams or 1½ oz)
1 Cup/Handful of Lettuce Leaves (40 grams or 1½ oz)
1 Cup/Handful of Avocado slices (120 grams or 4 oz)
150 ml / 5 fl oz of Hazelnut Milk

Protein 5g, Fat 20g, Carb 8g, Fibre 12g, 259 Kcals

Preparation

Put all the solid ingredients into the Tall Cup and press them down below the Max Line. Add the fluid base to fill the cup up to the Max Line. Screw the Nutribullet Extractor Blade on to the top of the cup. Invert the cup, press it down into the Nutribullet Power Base and twist it into place. Blast the mixture until it is really smooth (20 or so seconds). **Enjoy!**

Red Cabbage and Raspberry Nectar

Ingredients

1 Cup/Handful of Red or White Cabbage (40 grams or 1½ oz)
1 Cup/Handful of Broccoli Florets (40 grams or 1½ oz)
½ Cup of Raspberries (60 grams or 2 oz)
½ Cup of Avocado slices (60 grams or 2 oz)
150 ml / 5 fl oz of Almond Milk (Unsweetened)

Protein 4g, Fat 11g, Carb 8g, Fibre 10g, 172 Kcals

Preparation

Put all the solid ingredients into the Tall Cup and press them down below the Max Line. Add the fluid base to fill the cup up to the Max Line. Screw the Nutribullet Extractor Blade on to the top of the cup. Invert the cup, press it down into the Nutribullet Power Base and twist it into place. Blast the mixture until it is really smooth (20 or so seconds). **Enjoy!**

Verdant Chorus

Ingredients

1 Cup/Handful of Spinach (40 grams or 1½ oz)
1 Cup/Handful of Bok Choy (40 grams or 1½ oz)
1 Cup/Handful of Avocado slices (120 grams or 4 oz)
75 ml / 2½ fl oz of Coconut Milk
75 ml / 2½ fl oz of Greek Yoghurt

Protein 7g, Fat 26g, Carb 9g, Fibre 9g, 315 Kcals

Preparation

Put all the solid ingredients into the Tall Cup and press them down below the Max Line. Add the fluid base to fill the cup up to the Max Line. Screw the Nutribullet Extractor Blade on to the top of the cup. Invert the cup, press it down into the Nutribullet Power Base and twist it into place. Blast the mixture until it is really smooth (20 or so seconds). **Enjoy!**

Rocket needs Tangerine

Ingredients

1 Cup/Handful of Mint (40 grams or 1½ oz)
1 Cup/Handful of Rocket/Arugura Lettuce (40 grams or 1½ oz)
½ Cup of Tangerine slices (60 grams or 2 oz)
½ Cup of Avocado slices (60 grams or 2 oz)
150 ml / 5 fl oz of Almond Milk (Unsweetened)

Protein 4g, Fat 11g, Carb 9g, Fibre 9g, 170 Kcals

Preparation

Put all the solid ingredients into the Tall Cup and press them down below the Max Line. Add the fluid base to fill the cup up to the Max Line. Screw the Nutribullet Extractor Blade on to the top of the cup. Invert the cup, press it down into the Nutribullet Power Base and twist it into place. Blast the mixture until it is really smooth (20 or so seconds). **Enjoy!**

Lettuce and Strawberry Rapture

Ingredients

1 Cup/Handful of Bok Choy (40 grams or 1½ oz)
1 Cup/Handful of Lettuce Leaves (40 grams or 1½ oz)
½ Cup of Strawberries (60 grams or 2 oz)
½ Cup of Avocado slices (60 grams or 2 oz)
150 ml / 5 fl oz of Coconut Milk

Protein 3g, Fat 11g, Carb 10g, Fibre 6g, 157 Kcals

Preparation

Put all the solid ingredients into the Tall Cup and press them down below the Max Line. Add the fluid base to fill the cup up to the Max Line. Screw the Nutribullet Extractor Blade on to the top of the cup. Invert the cup, press it down into the Nutribullet Power Base and twist it into place. Blast the mixture until it is really smooth (20 or so seconds). **Enjoy!**

Peach Paradox

Ingredients

1 Cup/Handful of Green Cabbage (40 grams or 1½ oz)
1 Cup/Handful of Black Kale de-stemmed (40 grams or 1½ oz)
½ Cup of Blackberries (60 grams or 2 oz)
½ Cup of Peach slices (60 grams or 2 oz)
150 ml / 5 fl oz of Almond Milk (Unsweetened)

Protein 4g, Fat 3g, Carb 10g, Fibre 7g, 92 Kcals

Preparation

Put all the solid ingredients into the Tall Cup and press them down below the Max Line. Add the fluid base to fill the cup up to the Max Line. Screw the Nutribullet Extractor Blade on to the top of the cup. Invert the cup, press it down into the Nutribullet Power Base and twist it into place. Blast the mixture until it is really smooth (20 or so seconds). **Enjoy!**

Rocket goes Orange

Ingredients

1 Cup/Handful of Rocket/Arugura Lettuce (40 grams or 1½ oz)
1 Cup/Handful of Black Kale de-stemmed (40 grams or 1½ oz)
½ Cup of Blackberries (60 grams or 2 oz)
½ Cup of Orange segments (60 grams or 2 oz)
150 ml / 5 fl oz of Almond Milk (Unsweetened)

Protein 4g, Fat 3g, Carb 10g, Fibre 7g, 93 Kcals

Preparation

Put all the solid ingredients into the Tall Cup and press them down below the Max Line. Add the fluid base to fill the cup up to the Max Line. Screw the Nutribullet Extractor Blade on to the top of the cup. Invert the cup, press it down into the Nutribullet Power Base and twist it into place. Blast the mixture until it is really smooth (20 or so seconds). **Enjoy!**

Spinach and Avocado Concerto

Ingredients

1 Cup/Handful of Spinach (40 grams or 1½ oz)
1 Cup/Handful of Mint (40 grams or 1½ oz)
1 Cup/Handful of Avocado slices (120 grams or 4 oz)
75 ml / 2½ fl oz of Hazelnut Milk
75 ml / 2½ fl oz of Greek Yoghurt

Protein 8g, Fat 26g, Carb 10g, Fibre 12g, 334 Kcals

Preparation

Put all the solid ingredients into the Tall Cup and press them down below the Max Line. Add the fluid base to fill the cup up to the Max Line. Screw the Nutribullet Extractor Blade on to the top of the cup. Invert the cup, press it down into the Nutribullet Power Base and twist it into place. Blast the mixture until it is really smooth (20 or so seconds). **Enjoy!**

Fruity Waistline

Ingredients

2 Cups/Handfuls of Spinach (80 grams or 3 oz)
½ Cup of Avocado slices (60 grams or 2 oz)
½ Cup of Raspberries (60 grams or 2 oz)
150 ml / 5 fl oz of Hazelnut Milk

Protein 5g, Fat 12g, Carb 10g, Fibre 10g, 189 Kcals

Preparation

Put all the solid ingredients into the Tall Cup and press them down below the Max Line. Add the fluid base to fill the cup up to the Max Line. Screw the Nutribullet Extractor Blade on to the top of the cup. Invert the cup, press it down into the Nutribullet Power Base and twist it into place. Blast the mixture until it is really smooth (20 or so seconds). **Enjoy!**

Mint meets Nectarine

Ingredients

2 Cups/Handfuls of Mint (80 grams or 3 oz)
½ Cup of Nectarine segments (60 grams or 2 oz)
½ Cup of Raspberries (60 grams or 2 oz)
150 ml / 5 fl oz of Almond Milk (Unsweetened)

Protein 5g, Fat 3g, Carb 10g, Fibre 11g, 112 Kcals

Preparation

Put all the solid ingredients into the Tall Cup and press them down below the Max Line. Add the fluid base to fill the cup up to the Max Line. Screw the Nutribullet Extractor Blade on to the top of the cup. Invert the cup, press it down into the Nutribullet Power Base and twist it into place. Blast the mixture until it is really smooth (20 or so seconds). **Enjoy!**

Watercress and Cranberry Blend

Ingredients

2 Cups/Handfuls of Watercress (80 grams or 3 oz)
½ Cup of Avocado slices (60 grams or 2 oz)
½ Cup of Cranberries (60 grams or 2 oz)
150 ml / 5 fl oz of Coconut Milk

Protein 3g, Fat 10g, Carb 10g, Fibre 7g, 162 Kcals

Preparation

Put all the solid ingredients into the Tall Cup and press them down below the Max Line. Add the fluid base to fill the cup up to the Max Line. Screw the Nutribullet Extractor Blade on to the top of the cup. Invert the cup, press it down into the Nutribullet Power Base and twist it into place. Blast the mixture until it is really smooth (20 or so seconds). **Enjoy!**

Watercress and Peach Forever

Ingredients

2 Cups/Handfuls of Watercress (80 grams or 3 oz)
1 Cup/Handful of Peach slices (120 grams or 4 oz)
150 ml / 5 fl oz of Almond Milk (Unsweetened)

Protein 4g, Fat 2g, Carb 10g, Fibre 3g, 75 Kcals

Preparation

Put all the solid ingredients into the Tall Cup and press them down below the Max Line. Add the fluid base to fill the cup up to the Max Line. Screw the Nutribullet Extractor Blade on to the top of the cup. Invert the cup, press it down into the Nutribullet Power Base and twist it into place. Blast the mixture until it is really smooth (20 or so seconds). **Enjoy!**

Rocket loves Cranberry

Ingredients

2 Cups/Handfuls of Rocket/Arugura Lettuce (80 grams or 3 oz)
1 Cup/Handful of Cranberries (120 grams or 4 oz)
150 ml / 5 fl oz of Almond Milk (Unsweetened)

Protein 2g, Fat 2g, Carb 11g, Fibre 7g, 86 Kcals

Preparation

Put all the solid ingredients into the Tall Cup and press them down below the Max Line. Add the fluid base to fill the cup up to the Max Line. Screw the Nutribullet Extractor Blade on to the top of the cup. Invert the cup, press it down into the Nutribullet Power Base and twist it into place. Blast the mixture until it is really smooth (20 or so seconds). **Enjoy!**

Watercress joins Melon

Ingredients

2 Cups/Handfuls of Watercress (80 grams or 3 oz)
1 Cup/Handful of Melon chunks (120 grams or 8 oz)
150 ml / 5 fl oz of Almond Milk (Unsweetened)

Protein 3g, Fat 2g, Carb 11g, Fibre 2g, 71 Kcals

Preparation

Put all the solid ingredients into the Tall Cup and press them down below the Max Line. Add the fluid base to fill the cup up to the Max Line. Screw the Nutribullet Extractor Blade on to the top of the cup. Invert the cup, press it down into the Nutribullet Power Base and twist it into place. Blast the mixture until it is really smooth (20 or so seconds). **Enjoy!**

Watercress embraces Kiwi

Ingredients

1 Cup/Handful of Black Kale de-stemmed (40 grams or 1½ oz)
1 Cup/Handful of Watercress (40 grams or 1½ oz)
½ Cup of Kiwi Fruit slices (60 grams or 2 oz)
½ Cup of Blackberries (60 grams or 2 oz)
150 ml / 5 fl oz of Almond Milk (Unsweetened)

Protein 4g, Fat 3g, Carb 11g, Fibre 7g, 100 Kcals

Preparation

Put all the solid ingredients into the Tall Cup and press them down below the Max Line. Add the fluid base to fill the cup up to the Max Line. Screw the Nutribullet Extractor Blade on to the top of the cup. Invert the cup, press it down into the Nutribullet Power Base and twist it into place. Blast the mixture until it is really smooth (20 or so seconds). **Enjoy!**

Bok Choy and Blackberry Vortex

Ingredients

1 Cup/Handful of Rocket/Arugura Lettuce (40 grams or 1½ oz)
1 Cup/Handful of Bok Choy (40 grams or 1½ oz)
1 Cup/Handful of Blackberries (120 grams or 4 oz)
150 ml / 5 fl oz of Hazelnut Milk

Protein 3g, Fat 3g, Carb 11g, Fibre 8g, 106 Kcals

Preparation

Put all the solid ingredients into the Tall Cup and press them down below the Max Line. Add the fluid base to fill the cup up to the Max Line. Screw the Nutribullet Extractor Blade on to the top of the cup. Invert the cup, press it down into the Nutribullet Power Base and twist it into place. Blast the mixture until it is really smooth (20 or so seconds). **Enjoy!**

Rocket and Orange Detente

Ingredients

1 Cup/Handful of Rocket/Arugura Lettuce (40 grams or 1½ oz)
1 Cup/Handful of Green Cabbage (40 grams or 1½ oz)
½ Cup of Raspberries (60 grams or 2 oz)
½ Cup of Orange segments (60 grams or 2 oz)
150 ml / 5 fl oz of Almond Milk (Unsweetened)

Protein 3g, Fat 2g, Carb 11g, Fibre 7g, 94 Kcals

Preparation

Put all the solid ingredients into the Tall Cup and press them down below the Max Line. Add the fluid base to fill the cup up to the Max Line. Screw the Nutribullet Extractor Blade on to the top of the cup. Invert the cup, press it down into the Nutribullet Power Base and twist it into place. Blast the mixture until it is really smooth (20 or so seconds). *Enjoy!*

Ulra Low Carb Fruit and Veggie Blasts
Carbs are the poison exercise is the antidote (With Carb Grams)

Fennel joins Pecan

Ingredients

1 Cup/Handful of Black Kale de-stemmed (40 grams or 1½ oz)
1 Cup/Handful of Fennel (40 grams or 1½ oz)
½ Cup of Avocado slices (60 grams or 2 oz)
1 Cup/Handful of sliced Asparagus (120 grams or 4 oz)
30 grams or 1 oz of Pecans
150 ml / 5 fl oz of Almond Milk (Unsweetened)

Protein 9g, Fat 33g, Carb 7g, Fibre 12g, 373 Kcals

Preparation

Place the nuts or seeds into the Tall Cup. Screw the Nutribullet Extractor Blade on to the top of the cup. Invert the cup, press it down into the Nutribullet Power Base and twist it into place. Blast them for 30 seconds. Put the rest of the solid ingredients into the cup and press them down below the Max Line. Add the fluid base to fill the cup up to the Max Line. Screw the Nutribullet Extractor Blade on to the top of the cup. Invert the cup, press it down into the Nutribullet Power Base and twist it into place. Blast the mixture until it is really smooth (20 or so seconds). *Enjoy!*

Verdant Soother

Ingredients

2 Cups/Handfuls of Spinach (80 grams or 3 oz)
½ Cup of Avocado slices (60 grams or 2 oz)
1 Cup/Handful of sliced Fine Beans (120 grams or 4 oz)
30 grams or 1 oz of Brazil nuts
150 ml / 5 fl oz of Almond Milk (Unsweetened)

Protein 11g, Fat 31g, Carb 8g, Fibre 11g, 361 Kcals

Preparation

Place the nuts or seeds into the Tall Cup. Screw the Nutribullet Extractor Blade on to the top of the cup. Invert the cup, press it down into the Nutribullet Power Base and twist it into place. Blast them for 30 seconds. Put the rest of the solid ingredients into the cup and press them down below the Max Line. Add the fluid base to fill the cup up to the Max Line. Screw the Nutribullet Extractor Blade on to the top of the cup. Invert the cup, press it down into the Nutribullet Power Base and twist it into place. Blast the mixture until it is really smooth (20 or so seconds). **Enjoy!**

Fruity Rocker

Ingredients

1 Cup/Handful of Watercress (40 grams or 1½ oz)
1 Cup/Handful of Black Kale de-stemmed (40 grams or 1½ oz)
½ Cup of Avocado slices (60 grams or 2 oz)
1 Cup/Handful of sliced Tomato (120 grams or 4 oz)
30 grams or 1 oz of Hazelnuts
150 ml / 5 fl oz of Almond Milk (Unsweetened)

Protein 10g, Fat 30g, Carb 8g, Fibre 10g, 343 Kcals

Preparation

Place the nuts or seeds into the Tall Cup. Screw the Nutribullet Extractor Blade on to the top of the cup. Invert the cup, press it down into the Nutribullet Power Base and twist it into place. Blast them for 30 seconds. Put the rest of the solid ingredients into the cup and press them down below the Max Line. Add the fluid base to fill the cup up to the Max Line. Screw the Nutribullet Extractor Blade on to the top of the cup. Invert the cup, press it down into the Nutribullet Power Base and twist it into place. Blast the mixture until it is really smooth (20 or so seconds). **Enjoy!**

Veggie Elixir

Ingredients

2 Cups/Handfuls of Bok Choy (80 grams or 3 oz)
½ Cup of Blackberries (60 grams or 2 oz)
1 Cup/Handful of sliced Fine Beans (120 grams or 4 oz)
22 grams or ¾ oz of Sesame Seeds Hulled
150 ml / 5 fl oz of Almond Milk (Unsweetened)

Protein 9g, Fat 15g, Carb 8g, Fibre 9g, 217 Kcals

Preparation

Place the nuts or seeds into the Tall Cup. Screw the Nutribullet Extractor Blade on to the top of the cup. Invert the cup, press it down into the Nutribullet Power Base and twist it into place. Blast them for 30 seconds. Put the rest of the solid ingredients into the cup and press them down below the Max Line. Add the fluid base to fill the cup up to the Max Line. Screw the Nutribullet Extractor Blade on to the top of the cup. Invert the cup, press it down into the Nutribullet Power Base and twist it into place. Blast the mixture until it is really smooth (20 or so seconds). *Enjoy!*

Green Cabbage embraces Peanut

Ingredients

2 Cups/Handfuls of Green Cabbage (80 grams or 3 oz)
½ Cup of Avocado slices (60 grams or 2 oz)
1 Cup/Handful of sliced Celery (120 grams or 4 oz)
30 grams or 1 oz of Peanuts
150 ml / 5 fl oz of Almond Milk (Unsweetened)

Protein 11g, Fat 26g, Carb 8g, Fibre 11g, 324 Kcals

Preparation

Place the nuts or seeds into the Tall Cup. Screw the Nutribullet Extractor Blade on to the top of the cup. Invert the cup, press it down into the Nutribullet Power Base and twist it into place. Blast them for 30 seconds. Put the rest of the solid ingredients into the cup and press them down below the Max Line. Add the fluid base to fill the cup up to the Max Line. Screw the Nutribullet Extractor Blade on to the top of the cup. Invert the cup, press it down into the Nutribullet Power Base and twist it into place. Blast the mixture until it is really smooth (20 or so seconds). *Enjoy!*

Grapefruit in Flax

Ingredients

1 Cup/Handful of Watercress (40 grams or 1½ oz)
1 Cup/Handful of Bok Choy (40 grams or 1½ oz)
½ Cup of Grapefruit segments (60 grams or 2 oz)
1 Cup/Handful of sliced Zucchini/Courgette (120 grams or 4 oz)
22 grams or ¾ oz of Flax Seeds
150 ml / 5 fl oz of Almond Milk (Unsweetened)

Protein 8g, Fat 11g, Carb 8g, Fibre 9g, 186 Kcals

Preparation

Place the nuts or seeds into the Tall Cup. Screw the Nutribullet Extractor Blade on to the top of the cup. Invert the cup, press it down into the Nutribullet Power Base and twist it into place. Blast them for 30 seconds. Put the rest of the solid ingredients into the cup and press them down below the Max Line. Add the fluid base to fill the cup up to the Max Line. Screw the Nutribullet Extractor Blade on to the top of the cup. Invert the cup, press it down into the Nutribullet Power Base and twist it into place. Blast the mixture until it is really smooth (20 or so seconds). **Enjoy!**

Avocado and Walnut Refrain

Ingredients

1 Cup/Handful of Mint (40 grams or 1½ oz)
1 Cup/Handful of Lettuce Leaves (40 grams or 1½ oz)
½ Cup of Avocado slices (60 grams or 2 oz)
1 Cup/Handful of sliced Cauliflower florets (120 grams or 4 oz)
30 grams or 1 oz of Walnuts
150 ml / 5 fl oz of Almond Milk (Unsweetened)

Protein 10g, Fat 31g, Carb 8g, Fibre 13g, 366 Kcals

Preparation

Place the nuts or seeds into the Tall Cup. Screw the Nutribullet Extractor Blade on to the top of the cup. Invert the cup, press it down into the Nutribullet Power Base and twist it into place. Blast them for 30 seconds. Put the rest of the solid ingredients into the cup and press them down below the Max Line. Add the fluid base to fill the cup up to the Max Line. Screw the Nutribullet Extractor Blade on to the top of the cup. Invert the cup, press it down into the Nutribullet Power Base and twist it into place. Blast the mixture until it is really smooth (20 or so seconds). **Enjoy!**

Fennel and Almond Session

Ingredients

1 Cup/Handful of Fennel (40 grams or 1½ oz)
1 Cup/Handful of Green Cabbage (40 grams or 1½ oz)
½ Cup of Avocado slices (60 grams or 2 oz)
1 Cup/Handful of sliced Cucumber (120 grams or 4 oz)
30 grams or 1 oz of Almonds
150 ml / 5 fl oz of Almond Milk (Unsweetened)

Protein 10g, Fat 27g, Carb 8g, Fibre 11g, 329 Kcals

Preparation

Place the nuts or seeds into the Tall Cup. Screw the Nutribullet Extractor Blade on to the top of the cup. Invert the cup, press it down into the Nutribullet Power Base and twist it into place. Blast them for 30 seconds. Put the rest of the solid ingredients into the cup and press them down below the Max Line. Add the fluid base to fill the cup up to the Max Line. Screw the Nutribullet Extractor Blade on to the top of the cup. Invert the cup, press it down into the Nutribullet Power Base and twist it into place. Blast the mixture until it is really smooth (20 or so seconds). **Enjoy!**

Verdant Rejuvenator

Ingredients

1 Cup/Handful of Black Kale de-stemmed (40 grams or 1½ oz)
1 Cup/Handful of Bok Choy (40 grams or 1½ oz)
½ Cup of Avocado slices (60 grams or 2 oz)
1 Cup/Handful of sliced Cucumber (120 grams or 4 oz)
22 grams or ¾ oz of Sesame Seeds Hulled
150 ml / 5 fl oz of Coconut Milk

Protein 8g, Fat 24g, Carb 8g, Fibre 8g, 291 Kcals

Preparation

Place the nuts or seeds into the Tall Cup. Screw the Nutribullet Extractor Blade on to the top of the cup. Invert the cup, press it down into the Nutribullet Power Base and twist it into place. Blast them for 30 seconds. Put the rest of the solid ingredients into the cup and press them down below the Max Line. Add the fluid base to fill the cup up to the Max Line. Screw the Nutribullet Extractor Blade on to the top of the cup. Invert the cup, press it down into the Nutribullet Power Base and twist it into place. Blast the mixture until it is really smooth (20 or so seconds). **Enjoy!**

Orange meets Flax

Ingredients

1 Cup/Handful of Lettuce Leaves (40 grams or 1½ oz)
1 Cup/Handful of Watercress (40 grams or 1½ oz)
½ Cup of Orange segments (60 grams or 2 oz)
1 Cup/Handful of sliced Celery (120 grams or 4 oz)
22 grams or ¾ oz of Flax Seeds
150 ml / 5 fl oz of Almond Milk (Unsweetened)

Protein 7g, Fat 11g, Carb 9g, Fibre 11g, 195 Kcals

Preparation

Place the nuts or seeds into the Tall Cup. Screw the Nutribullet Extractor Blade on to the top of the cup. Invert the cup, press it down into the Nutribullet Power Base and twist it into place. Blast them for 30 seconds. Put the rest of the solid ingredients into the cup and press them down below the Max Line. Add the fluid base to fill the cup up to the Max Line. Screw the Nutribullet Extractor Blade on to the top of the cup. Invert the cup, press it down into the Nutribullet Power Base and twist it into place. Blast the mixture until it is really smooth (20 or so seconds). ***Enjoy!***

Green Blossom

Ingredients

1 Cup/Handful of Broccoli Florets (40 grams or 1½ oz)
1 Cup/Handful of Rocket/Arugura Lettuce (40 grams or 1½ oz)
½ Cup of Blackberries (60 grams or 2 oz)
1 Cup/Handful of sliced Celery (120 grams or 4 oz)
22 grams or ¾ oz of Pumpkin Seeds
150 ml / 5 fl oz of Almond Milk (Unsweetened)

Protein 9g, Fat 12g, Carb 9g, Fibre 8g, 208 Kcals

Preparation

Place the nuts or seeds into the Tall Cup. Screw the Nutribullet Extractor Blade on to the top of the cup. Invert the cup, press it down into the Nutribullet Power Base and twist it into place. Blast them for 30 seconds. Put the rest of the solid ingredients into the cup and press them down below the Max Line. Add the fluid base to fill the cup up to the Max Line. Screw the Nutribullet Extractor Blade on to the top of the cup. Invert the cup, press it down into the Nutribullet Power Base and twist it into place. Blast the mixture until it is really smooth (20 or so seconds). ***Enjoy!***

Verdant Sunshine

Ingredients

1 Cup/Handful of Watercress (40 grams or 1½ oz)
1 Cup/Handful of Rocket/Arugura Lettuce (40 grams or 1½ oz)
½ Cup of Orange segments (60 grams or 2 oz)
1 Cup/Handful of sliced Cucumber (120 grams or 4 oz)
22 grams or ¾ oz of Flax Seeds
150 ml / 5 fl oz of Almond Milk (Unsweetened)

Protein 7g, Fat 11g, Carb 9g, Fibre 10g, 189 Kcals

Preparation

Place the nuts or seeds into the Tall Cup. Screw the Nutribullet Extractor Blade on to the top of the cup. Invert the cup, press it down into the Nutribullet Power Base and twist it into place. Blast them for 30 seconds. Put the rest of the solid ingredients into the cup and press them down below the Max Line. Add the fluid base to fill the cup up to the Max Line. Screw the Nutribullet Extractor Blade on to the top of the cup. Invert the cup, press it down into the Nutribullet Power Base and twist it into place. Blast the mixture until it is really smooth (20 or so seconds). **Enjoy!**

Watercress embraces Apricot

Ingredients

1 Cup/Handful of Spinach (40 grams or 1½ oz)
1 Cup/Handful of Watercress (40 grams or 1½ oz)
½ Cup of Apricot halves (60 grams or 2 oz)
1 Cup/Handful of sliced Zucchini/Courgette (120 grams or 4 oz)
22 grams or ¾ oz of Flax Seeds
150 ml / 5 fl oz of Almond Milk (Unsweetened)

Protein 9g, Fat 12g, Carb 9g, Fibre 10g, 199 Kcals

Preparation

Place the nuts or seeds into the Tall Cup. Screw the Nutribullet Extractor Blade on to the top of the cup. Invert the cup, press it down into the Nutribullet Power Base and twist it into place. Blast them for 30 seconds. Put the rest of the solid ingredients into the cup and press them down below the Max Line. Add the fluid base to fill the cup up to the Max Line. Screw the Nutribullet Extractor Blade on to the top of the cup. Invert the cup, press it down into the Nutribullet Power Base and twist it into place. Blast the mixture until it is really smooth (20 or so seconds). **Enjoy!**

Rocket and Cranberry Vision

Ingredients

2 Cups/Handfuls of Rocket/Arugura Lettuce (80 grams or 3 oz)
½ Cup of Cranberries (60 grams or 2 oz)
1 Cup/Handful of sliced Asparagus (120 grams or 4 oz)
30 grams or 1 oz of Pecans
150 ml / 5 fl oz of Almond Milk (Unsweetened)

Protein 7g, Fat 24g, Carb 9g, Fibre 10g, 290 Kcals

Preparation

Place the nuts or seeds into the Tall Cup. Screw the Nutribullet Extractor Blade on to the top of the cup. Invert the cup, press it down into the Nutribullet Power Base and twist it into place. Blast them for 30 seconds. Put the rest of the solid ingredients into the cup and press them down below the Max Line. Add the fluid base to fill the cup up to the Max Line. Screw the Nutribullet Extractor Blade on to the top of the cup. Invert the cup, press it down into the Nutribullet Power Base and twist it into place. Blast the mixture until it is really smooth (20 or so seconds). **Enjoy!**

Black Kale joins Pecan

Ingredients

1 Cup/Handful of Black Kale de-stemmed (40 grams or 1½ oz)
1 Cup/Handful of Lettuce Leaves (40 grams or 1½ oz)
½ Cup of Avocado slices (60 grams or 2 oz)
1 Cup/Handful of Radishes (120 grams or 4 oz)
30 grams or 1 oz of Pecans
150 ml / 5 fl oz of Coconut Milk

Protein 7g, Fat 33g, Carb 10g, Fibre 11g, 373 Kcals

Preparation

Place the nuts or seeds into the Tall Cup. Screw the Nutribullet Extractor Blade on to the top of the cup. Invert the cup, press it down into the Nutribullet Power Base and twist it into place. Blast them for 30 seconds. Put the rest of the solid ingredients into the cup and press them down below the Max Line. Add the fluid base to fill the cup up to the Max Line. Screw the Nutribullet Extractor Blade on to the top of the cup. Invert the cup, press it down into the Nutribullet Power Base and twist it into place. Blast the mixture until it is really smooth (20 or so seconds). **Enjoy!**

Red Cabbage meets Pumpkin

Ingredients

2 Cups/Handfuls of Red or White Cabbage (80 grams or 3 oz)
½ Cup of Avocado slices (60 grams or 2 oz)
1 Cup/Handful of sliced Asparagus (120 grams or 4 oz)
22 grams or ¾ oz of Pumpkin Seeds
150 ml / 5 fl oz of Almond Milk (Unsweetened)

Protein 11g, Fat 20g, Carb 10g, Fibre 10g, 288 Kcals

Preparation

Place the nuts or seeds into the Tall Cup. Screw the Nutribullet Extractor Blade on to the top of the cup. Invert the cup, press it down into the Nutribullet Power Base and twist it into place. Blast them for 30 seconds. Put the rest of the solid ingredients into the cup and press them down below the Max Line. Add the fluid base to fill the cup up to the Max Line. Screw the Nutribullet Extractor Blade on to the top of the cup. Invert the cup, press it down into the Nutribullet Power Base and twist it into place. Blast the mixture until it is really smooth (20 or so seconds). **Enjoy!**

Fennel on Peanut

Ingredients

1 Cup/Handful of Watercress (40 grams or 1½ oz)
1 Cup/Handful of Fennel (40 grams or 1½ oz)
½ Cup of Raspberries (60 grams or 2 oz)
1 Cup/Handful of Radishes (120 grams or 4 oz)
30 grams or 1 oz of Peanuts
150 ml / 5 fl oz of Almond Milk (Unsweetened)

Protein 11g, Fat 17g, Carb 10g, Fibre 10g, 256 Kcals

Preparation

Place the nuts or seeds into the Tall Cup. Screw the Nutribullet Extractor Blade on to the top of the cup. Invert the cup, press it down into the Nutribullet Power Base and twist it into place. Blast them for 30 seconds. Put the rest of the solid ingredients into the cup and press them down below the Max Line. Add the fluid base to fill the cup up to the Max Line. Screw the Nutribullet Extractor Blade on to the top of the cup. Invert the cup, press it down into the Nutribullet Power Base and twist it into place. Blast the mixture until it is really smooth (20 or so seconds). **Enjoy!**

Clementine needs Flax

Ingredients

1 Cup/Handful of Spinach (40 grams or 1½ oz)
1 Cup/Handful of Lettuce Leaves (40 grams or 1½ oz)
½ Cup of Clementine slices (60 grams or 2 oz)
1 Cup/Handful of Radishes (120 grams or 4 oz)
22 grams or ¾ oz of Flax Seeds
150 ml / 5 fl oz of Almond Milk (Unsweetened)

Protein 8g, Fat 11g, Carb 10g, Fibre 11g, 200 Kcals

Preparation

Place the nuts or seeds into the Tall Cup. Screw the Nutribullet Extractor Blade on to the top of the cup. Invert the cup, press it down into the Nutribullet Power Base and twist it into place. Blast them for 30 seconds. Put the rest of the solid ingredients into the cup and press them down below the Max Line. Add the fluid base to fill the cup up to the Max Line. Screw the Nutribullet Extractor Blade on to the top of the cup. Invert the cup, press it down into the Nutribullet Power Base and twist it into place. Blast the mixture until it is really smooth (20 or so seconds). **Enjoy!**

Lettuce loves Cranberry

Ingredients

1 Cup/Handful of Lettuce Leaves (40 grams or 1½ oz)
1 Cup/Handful of Spinach (40 grams or 1½ oz)
½ Cup of Cranberries (60 grams or 2 oz)
1 Cup/Handful of sliced Zucchini/Courgette (120 grams or 4 oz)
22 grams or ¾ oz of Chia Seeds
150 ml / 5 fl oz of Almond Milk (Unsweetened)

Protein 8g, Fat 9g, Carb 10g, Fibre 14g, 190 Kcals

Preparation

Place the nuts or seeds into the Tall Cup. Screw the Nutribullet Extractor Blade on to the top of the cup. Invert the cup, press it down into the Nutribullet Power Base and twist it into place. Blast them for 30 seconds. Put the rest of the solid ingredients into the cup and press them down below the Max Line. Add the fluid base to fill the cup up to the Max Line. Screw the Nutribullet Extractor Blade on to the top of the cup. Invert the cup, press it down into the Nutribullet Power Base and twist it into place. Blast the mixture until it is really smooth (20 or so seconds). **Enjoy!**

Papaya and Cucumber Delusion

Ingredients

2 Cups/Handfuls of Lettuce Leaves (80 grams or 3 oz)
½ Cup of Papaya (60 grams or 2 oz)
1 Cup/Handful of sliced Cucumber (120 grams or 4 oz)
22 grams or ¾ oz of Chia Seeds
150 ml / 5 fl oz of Almond Milk (Unsweetened)

Protein 6g, Fat 9g, Carb 10g, Fibre 12g, 180 Kcals

Preparation

Place the nuts or seeds into the Tall Cup. Screw the Nutribullet Extractor Blade on to the top of the cup. Invert the cup, press it down into the Nutribullet Power Base and twist it into place. Blast them for 30 seconds. Put the rest of the solid ingredients into the cup and press them down below the Max Line. Add the fluid base to fill the cup up to the Max Line. Screw the Nutribullet Extractor Blade on to the top of the cup. Invert the cup, press it down into the Nutribullet Power Base and twist it into place. Blast the mixture until it is really smooth (20 or so seconds). **Enjoy!**

Watercress and Grapefruit Regatta

Ingredients

1 Cup/Handful of Watercress (40 grams or 1½ oz)
1 Cup/Handful of Broccoli Florets (40 grams or 1½ oz)
½ Cup of Grapefruit segments (60 grams or 2 oz)
1 Cup/Handful of sliced Celery (120 grams or 4 oz)
30 grams or 1 oz of Hazelnuts
150 ml / 5 fl oz of Almond Milk (Unsweetened)

Protein 8g, Fat 20g, Carb 10g, Fibre 7g, 264 Kcals

Preparation

Place the nuts or seeds into the Tall Cup. Screw the Nutribullet Extractor Blade on to the top of the cup. Invert the cup, press it down into the Nutribullet Power Base and twist it into place. Blast them for 30 seconds. Put the rest of the solid ingredients into the cup and press them down below the Max Line. Add the fluid base to fill the cup up to the Max Line. Screw the Nutribullet Extractor Blade on to the top of the cup. Invert the cup, press it down into the Nutribullet Power Base and twist it into place. Blast the mixture until it is really smooth (20 or so seconds). **Enjoy!**

Blackberry in Cucumber

Ingredients

2 Cups/Handfuls of Fennel (80 grams or 3 oz)
½ Cup of Blackberries (60 grams or 2 oz)
1 Cup/Handful of sliced Cucumber (120 grams or 4 oz)
30 grams or 1 oz of Peanuts
150 ml / 5 fl oz of Almond Milk (Unsweetened)

Protein 11g, Fat 17g, Carb 10g, Fibre 10g, 254 Kcals

Preparation

Place the nuts or seeds into the Tall Cup. Screw the Nutribullet Extractor Blade on to the top of the cup. Invert the cup, press it down into the Nutribullet Power Base and twist it into place. Blast them for 30 seconds. Put the rest of the solid ingredients into the cup and press them down below the Max Line. Add the fluid base to fill the cup up to the Max Line. Screw the Nutribullet Extractor Blade on to the top of the cup. Invert the cup, press it down into the Nutribullet Power Base and twist it into place. Blast the mixture until it is really smooth (20 or so seconds). **Enjoy!**

Tangerine Treat

Ingredients

2 Cups/Handfuls of Spinach (80 grams or 3 oz)
½ Cup of Tangerine slices (60 grams or 2 oz)
1 Cup/Handful of sliced Cucumber (120 grams or 4 oz)
22 grams or ¾ oz of Sesame Seeds Hulled
150 ml / 5 fl oz of Almond Milk (Unsweetened)

Protein 8g, Fat 15g, Carb 10g, Fibre 6g, 215 Kcals

Preparation

Place the nuts or seeds into the Tall Cup. Screw the Nutribullet Extractor Blade on to the top of the cup. Invert the cup, press it down into the Nutribullet Power Base and twist it into place. Blast them for 30 seconds. Put the rest of the solid ingredients into the cup and press them down below the Max Line. Add the fluid base to fill the cup up to the Max Line. Screw the Nutribullet Extractor Blade on to the top of the cup. Invert the cup, press it down into the Nutribullet Power Base and twist it into place. Blast the mixture until it is really smooth (20 or so seconds). **Enjoy!**

Green Dictator

Ingredients

1 Cup/Handful of Red or White Cabbage (40 grams or 1½ oz)
1 Cup/Handful of Lettuce Leaves (40 grams or 1½ oz)
½ Cup of Raspberries (60 grams or 2 oz)
1 Cup/Handful of sliced Zucchini/Courgette (120 grams or 4 oz)
22 grams or ¾ oz of Chia Seeds
150 ml / 5 fl oz of Almond Milk (Unsweetened)

Protein 7g, Fat 9g, Carb 10g, Fibre 15g, 197 Kcals

Preparation

Place the nuts or seeds into the Tall Cup. Screw the Nutribullet Extractor Blade on to the top of the cup. Invert the cup, press it down into the Nutribullet Power Base and twist it into place. Blast them for 30 seconds. Put the rest of the solid ingredients into the cup and press them down below the Max Line. Add the fluid base to fill the cup up to the Max Line. Screw the Nutribullet Extractor Blade on to the top of the cup. Invert the cup, press it down into the Nutribullet Power Base and twist it into place. Blast the mixture until it is really smooth (20 or so seconds). **Enjoy!**

Red Cabbage and Water Melon Guru

Ingredients

1 Cup/Handful of Red or White Cabbage (40 grams or 1½ oz)
1 Cup/Handful of Watercress (40 grams or 1½ oz)
½ Cup of Water Melon chunks (60 grams or 2 oz)
1 Cup/Handful of Radishes (120 grams or 4 oz)
30 grams or 1 oz of Pecans
150 ml / 5 fl oz of Almond Milk (Unsweetened)

Protein 6g, Fat 24g, Carb 10g, Fibre 7g, 280 Kcals

Preparation

Place the nuts or seeds into the Tall Cup. Screw the Nutribullet Extractor Blade on to the top of the cup. Invert the cup, press it down into the Nutribullet Power Base and twist it into place. Blast them for 30 seconds. Put the rest of the solid ingredients into the cup and press them down below the Max Line. Add the fluid base to fill the cup up to the Max Line. Screw the Nutribullet Extractor Blade on to the top of the cup. Invert the cup, press it down into the Nutribullet Power Base and twist it into place. Blast the mixture until it is really smooth (20 or so seconds). **Enjoy!**

Clementine Cascade

Ingredients

1 Cup/Handful of Lettuce Leaves (40 grams or 1½ oz)
1 Cup/Handful of Spinach (40 grams or 1½ oz)
½ Cup of Clementine slices (60 grams or 2 oz)
1 Cup/Handful of sliced Cucumber (120 grams or 4 oz)
30 grams or 1 oz of Pecans
150 ml / 5 fl oz of Almond Milk (Unsweetened)

Protein 6g, Fat 24g, Carb 10g, Fibre 7g, 285 Kcals

Preparation

Place the nuts or seeds into the Tall Cup. Screw the Nutribullet Extractor Blade on to the top of the cup. Invert the cup, press it down into the Nutribullet Power Base and twist it into place. Blast them for 30 seconds. Put the rest of the solid ingredients into the cup and press them down below the Max Line. Add the fluid base to fill the cup up to the Max Line. Screw the Nutribullet Extractor Blade on to the top of the cup. Invert the cup, press it down into the Nutribullet Power Base and twist it into place. Blast the mixture until it is really smooth (20 or so seconds). **Enjoy!**

Apricot and Zucchini Extravaganza

Ingredients

1 Cup/Handful of Bok Choy (40 grams or 1½ oz)
1 Cup/Handful of Spinach (40 grams or 1½ oz)
½ Cup of Apricot halves (60 grams or 2 oz)
1 Cup/Handful of sliced Zucchini/Courgette (120 grams or 4 oz)
30 grams or 1 oz of Brazil nuts
150 ml / 5 fl oz of Almond Milk (Unsweetened)

Protein 9g, Fat 23g, Carb 10g, Fibre 7g, 280 Kcals

Preparation

Place the nuts or seeds into the Tall Cup. Screw the Nutribullet Extractor Blade on to the top of the cup. Invert the cup, press it down into the Nutribullet Power Base and twist it into place. Blast them for 30 seconds. Put the rest of the solid ingredients into the cup and press them down below the Max Line. Add the fluid base to fill the cup up to the Max Line. Screw the Nutribullet Extractor Blade on to the top of the cup. Invert the cup, press it down into the Nutribullet Power Base and twist it into place. Blast the mixture until it is really smooth (20 or so seconds). **Enjoy!**

Verdant Gala

Ingredients

1 Cup/Handful of Black Kale de-stemmed (40 grams or 1½ oz)
1 Cup/Handful of Green Cabbage (40 grams or 1½ oz)
½ Cup of Raspberries (60 grams or 2 oz)
1 Cup/Handful of sliced Asparagus (120 grams or 4 oz)
22 grams or ¾ oz of Sunflower Seeds Hulled
150 ml / 5 fl oz of Almond Milk (Unsweetened)

Protein 10g, Fat 13g, Carb 10g, Fibre 10g, 212 Kcals

Preparation

Place the nuts or seeds into the Tall Cup. Screw the Nutribullet Extractor Blade on to the top of the cup. Invert the cup, press it down into the Nutribullet Power Base and twist it into place. Blast them for 30 seconds. Put the rest of the solid ingredients into the cup and press them down below the Max Line. Add the fluid base to fill the cup up to the Max Line. Screw the Nutribullet Extractor Blade on to the top of the cup. Invert the cup, press it down into the Nutribullet Power Base and twist it into place. Blast the mixture until it is really smooth (20 or so seconds). ***Enjoy!***

Green Cabbage and Walnut Orchestra

Ingredients

1 Cup/Handful of Green Cabbage (40 grams or 1½ oz)
1 Cup/Handful of Bok Choy (40 grams or 1½ oz)
½ Cup of Peach slices (60 grams or 2 oz)
1 Cup/Handful of sliced Celery (120 grams or 4 oz)
30 grams or 1 oz of Walnuts
150 ml / 5 fl oz of Almond Milk (Unsweetened)

Protein 8g, Fat 22g, Carb 11g, Fibre 7g, 273 Kcals

Preparation

Place the nuts or seeds into the Tall Cup. Screw the Nutribullet Extractor Blade on to the top of the cup. Invert the cup, press it down into the Nutribullet Power Base and twist it into place. Blast them for 30 seconds. Put the rest of the solid ingredients into the cup and press them down below the Max Line. Add the fluid base to fill the cup up to the Max Line. Screw the Nutribullet Extractor Blade on to the top of the cup. Invert the cup, press it down into the Nutribullet Power Base and twist it into place. Blast the mixture until it is really smooth (20 or so seconds). ***Enjoy!***

Bok Choy goes Almond

Ingredients

1 Cup/Handful of Rocket/Arugura Lettuce (40 grams or 1½ oz)
1 Cup/Handful of Bok Choy (40 grams or 1½ oz)
½ Cup of Avocado slices (60 grams or 2 oz)
1 Cup/Handful of sliced Asparagus (120 grams or 4 oz)
30 grams or 1 oz of Almonds
150 ml / 5 fl oz of Coconut Milk

Protein 11g, Fat 26g, Carb 11g, Fibre 10g, 338 Kcals

Preparation

Place the nuts or seeds into the Tall Cup. Screw the Nutribullet Extractor Blade on to the top of the cup. Invert the cup, press it down into the Nutribullet Power Base and twist it into place. Blast them for 30 seconds. Put the rest of the solid ingredients into the cup and press them down below the Max Line. Add the fluid base to fill the cup up to the Max Line. Screw the Nutribullet Extractor Blade on to the top of the cup. Invert the cup, press it down into the Nutribullet Power Base and twist it into place. Blast the mixture until it is really smooth (20 or so seconds). **Enjoy!**

Avocado meets Walnut

Ingredients

1 Cup/Handful of Bok Choy (40 grams or 1½ oz)
1 Cup/Handful of Mint (40 grams or 1½ oz)
½ Cup of Avocado slices (60 grams or 2 oz)
1 Cup/Handful of Radishes (120 grams or 4 oz)
30 grams or 1 oz of Walnuts
75 ml / 2½ fl oz of Almond Milk (Unsweetened)
75 ml / 2½ fl oz of Greek Yoghurt

Protein 12g, Fat 37g, Carb 11g, Fibre 11g, 437 Kcals

Preparation

Place the nuts or seeds into the Tall Cup. Screw the Nutribullet Extractor Blade on to the top of the cup. Invert the cup, press it down into the Nutribullet Power Base and twist it into place. Blast them for 30 seconds. Put the rest of the solid ingredients into the cup and press them down below the Max Line. Add the fluid base to fill the cup up to the Max Line. Screw the Nutribullet Extractor Blade on to the top of the cup. Invert the cup, press it down into the Nutribullet Power Base and twist it into place. Blast the mixture until it is really smooth (20 or so seconds). **Enjoy!**

Orange and Zucchini Power

Ingredients

2 Cups/Handfuls of Spinach (80 grams or 3 oz)
½ Cup of Orange segments (60 grams or 2 oz)
1 Cup/Handful of sliced Zucchini/Courgette (120 grams or 4 oz)
30 grams or 1 oz of Brazil nuts
150 ml / 5 fl oz of Almond Milk (Unsweetened)

Protein 9g, Fat 23g, Carb 11g, Fibre 7g, 284 Kcals

Preparation

Place the nuts or seeds into the Tall Cup. Screw the Nutribullet Extractor Blade on to the top of the cup. Invert the cup, press it down into the Nutribullet Power Base and twist it into place. Blast them for 30 seconds. Put the rest of the solid ingredients into the cup and press them down below the Max Line. Add the fluid base to fill the cup up to the Max Line. Screw the Nutribullet Extractor Blade on to the top of the cup. Invert the cup, press it down into the Nutribullet Power Base and twist it into place. Blast the mixture until it is really smooth (20 or so seconds). ***Enjoy!***

Black Kale joins Water Melon

Ingredients

1 Cup/Handful of Fennel (40 grams or 1½ oz)
1 Cup/Handful of Black Kale de-stemmed (40 grams or 1½ oz)
½ Cup of Water Melon chunks (60 grams or 2 oz)
1 Cup/Handful of sliced Cucumber (120 grams or 4 oz)
22 grams or ¾ oz of Pumpkin Seeds
150 ml / 5 fl oz of Almond Milk (Unsweetened)

Protein 9g, Fat 12g, Carb 11g, Fibre 5g, 202 Kcals

Preparation

Place the nuts or seeds into the Tall Cup. Screw the Nutribullet Extractor Blade on to the top of the cup. Invert the cup, press it down into the Nutribullet Power Base and twist it into place. Blast them for 30 seconds. Put the rest of the solid ingredients into the cup and press them down below the Max Line. Add the fluid base to fill the cup up to the Max Line. Screw the Nutribullet Extractor Blade on to the top of the cup. Invert the cup, press it down into the Nutribullet Power Base and twist it into place. Blast the mixture until it is really smooth (20 or so seconds). ***Enjoy!***

Lettuce loves Almond

Ingredients

1 Cup/Handful of Watercress (40 grams or 1½ oz)
1 Cup/Handful of Lettuce Leaves (40 grams or 1½ oz)
½ Cup of Raspberries (60 grams or 2 oz)
1 Cup/Handful of sliced Red Pepper (120 grams or 4 oz)
30 grams or 1 oz of Almonds
150 ml / 5 fl oz of Almond Milk (Unsweetened)

Protein 10g, Fat 18g, Carb 11g, Fibre 11g, 276 Kcals

Preparation

Place the nuts or seeds into the Tall Cup. Screw the Nutribullet Extractor Blade on to the top of the cup. Invert the cup, press it down into the Nutribullet Power Base and twist it into place. Blast them for 30 seconds. Put the rest of the solid ingredients into the cup and press them down below the Max Line. Add the fluid base to fill the cup up to the Max Line. Screw the Nutribullet Extractor Blade on to the top of the cup. Invert the cup, press it down into the Nutribullet Power Base and twist it into place. Blast the mixture until it is really smooth (20 or so seconds). **Enjoy!**

Mint in Chia

Ingredients

1 Cup/Handful of Mint (40 grams or 1½ oz)
1 Cup/Handful of Fennel (40 grams or 1½ oz)
½ Cup of Water Melon chunks (60 grams or 2 oz)
1 Cup/Handful of sliced Zucchini/Courgette (120 grams or 4 oz)
22 grams or ¾ oz of Chia Seeds
150 ml / 5 fl oz of Almond Milk (Unsweetened)

Protein 8g, Fat 9g, Carb 11g, Fibre 14g, 194 Kcals

Preparation

Place the nuts or seeds into the Tall Cup. Screw the Nutribullet Extractor Blade on to the top of the cup. Invert the cup, press it down into the Nutribullet Power Base and twist it into place. Blast them for 30 seconds. Put the rest of the solid ingredients into the cup and press them down below the Max Line. Add the fluid base to fill the cup up to the Max Line. Screw the Nutribullet Extractor Blade on to the top of the cup. Invert the cup, press it down into the Nutribullet Power Base and twist it into place. Blast the mixture until it is really smooth (20 or so seconds). **Enjoy!**

Bok Choy on Rocket

Ingredients

1 Cup/Handful of Bok Choy (40 grams or 1½ oz)
1 Cup/Handful of Rocket/Arugura Lettuce (40 grams or 1½ oz)
½ Cup of Avocado slices (60 grams or 2 oz)
1 Cup/Handful of sliced Cucumber (120 grams or 4 oz)
150 ml / 5 fl oz of Almond Milk (Unsweetened)

Protein 4g, Fat 11g, Carb 4g, Fibre 6g, 141 Kcals

Preparation

Put all the solid ingredients into the Tall Cup and press them down below the Max Line. Add the fluid base to fill the cup up to the Max Line. Screw the Nutribullet Extractor Blade on to the top of the cup. Invert the cup, press it down into the Nutribullet Power Base and twist it into place. Blast the mixture until it is really smooth (20 or so seconds). ***Enjoy!***

Green Cabbage needs Bok Choy

Ingredients

1 Cup/Handful of Green Cabbage (40 grams or 1½ oz)
1 Cup/Handful of Bok Choy (40 grams or 1½ oz)
½ Cup of Avocado slices (60 grams or 2 oz)
1 Cup/Handful of sliced Fine Beans (120 grams or 4 oz)
150 ml / 5 fl oz of Almond Milk (Unsweetened)

Protein 5g, Fat 11g, Carb 7g, Fibre 9g, 160 Kcals

Preparation

Put all the solid ingredients into the Tall Cup and press them down below the Max Line. Add the fluid base to fill the cup up to the Max Line. Screw the Nutribullet Extractor Blade on to the top of the cup. Invert the cup, press it down into the Nutribullet Power Base and twist it into place. Blast the mixture until it is really smooth (20 or so seconds). ***Enjoy!***

Green Salad

Ingredients

1 Cup/Handful of Rocket/Arugura Lettuce (40 grams or 1½ oz)
1 Cup/Handful of Lettuce Leaves (40 grams or 1½ oz)
½ Cup of Grapefruit segments (60 grams or 2 oz)
1 Cup/Handful of sliced Zucchini/Courgette (120 grams or 4 oz)
150 ml / 5 fl oz of Almond Milk (Unsweetened)

Protein 3g, Fat 2g, Carb 8g, Fibre 4g, 71 Kcals

Preparation

Put all the solid ingredients into the Tall Cup and press them down below the Max Line. Add the fluid base to fill the cup up to the Max Line. Screw the Nutribullet Extractor Blade on to the top of the cup. Invert the cup, press it down into the Nutribullet Power Base and twist it into place. Blast the mixture until it is really smooth (20 or so seconds). **Enjoy!**

Spinach embraces Rocket

Ingredients

1 Cup/Handful of Spinach (40 grams or 1½ oz)
1 Cup/Handful of Rocket/Arugura Lettuce (40 grams or 1½ oz)
½ Cup of Apricot halves (60 grams or 2 oz)
1 Cup/Handful of sliced Celery (120 grams or 4 oz)
150 ml / 5 fl oz of Almond Milk (Unsweetened)

Protein 4g, Fat 2g, Carb 8g, Fibre 5g, 82 Kcals

Preparation

Put all the solid ingredients into the Tall Cup and press them down below the Max Line. Add the fluid base to fill the cup up to the Max Line. Screw the Nutribullet Extractor Blade on to the top of the cup. Invert the cup, press it down into the Nutribullet Power Base and twist it into place. Blast the mixture until it is really smooth (20 or so seconds). **Enjoy!**

Black Kale goes Fennel

Ingredients

1 Cup/Handful of Black Kale de-stemmed (40 grams or 1½ oz)
1 Cup/Handful of Fennel (40 grams or 1½ oz)
½ Cup of Strawberries (60 grams or 2 oz)
1 Cup/Handful of sliced Zucchini/Courgette (120 grams or 4 oz)
150 ml / 5 fl oz of Almond Milk (Unsweetened)

Protein 4g, Fat 3g, Carb 8g, Fibre 5g, 85 Kcals

Preparation

Put all the solid ingredients into the Tall Cup and press them down below the Max Line. Add the fluid base to fill the cup up to the Max Line. Screw the Nutribullet Extractor Blade on to the top of the cup. Invert the cup, press it down into the Nutribullet Power Base and twist it into place. Blast the mixture until it is really smooth (20 or so seconds). *Enjoy!*

Lettuce and Nectarine Creation

Ingredients

1 Cup/Handful of Watercress (40 grams or 1½ oz)
1 Cup/Handful of Lettuce Leaves (40 grams or 1½ oz)
½ Cup of Nectarine segments (60 grams or 2 oz)
1 Cup/Handful of sliced Asparagus (120 grams or 4 oz)
150 ml / 5 fl oz of Almond Milk (Unsweetened)

Protein 5g, Fat 2g, Carb 9g, Fibre 5g, 81 Kcals

Preparation

Put all the solid ingredients into the Tall Cup and press them down below the Max Line. Add the fluid base to fill the cup up to the Max Line. Screw the Nutribullet Extractor Blade on to the top of the cup. Invert the cup, press it down into the Nutribullet Power Base and twist it into place. Blast the mixture until it is really smooth (20 or so seconds). *Enjoy!*

Fruity Revelation

Ingredients

1 Cup/Handful of Spinach (40 grams or 1½ oz)
1 Cup/Handful of Mint (40 grams or 1½ oz)
½ Cup of Avocado slices (60 grams or 2 oz)
1 Cup/Handful of Radishes (120 grams or 4 oz)
75 ml / 2½ fl oz of Almond Milk (Unsweetened)
75 ml / 2½ fl oz of Greek Yoghurt

Protein 8g, Fat 17g, Carb 9g, Fibre 10g, 245 Kcals

Preparation

Put all the solid ingredients into the Tall Cup and press them down below the Max Line. Add the fluid base to fill the cup up to the Max Line. Screw the Nutribullet Extractor Blade on to the top of the cup. Invert the cup, press it down into the Nutribullet Power Base and twist it into place. Blast the mixture until it is really smooth (20 or so seconds). **Enjoy!**

Mint and Green Cabbage Feast

Ingredients

1 Cup/Handful of Mint (40 grams or 1½ oz)
1 Cup/Handful of Green Cabbage (40 grams or 1½ oz)
½ Cup of Raspberries (60 grams or 2 oz)
1 Cup/Handful of sliced Cauliflower florets (120 grams or 4 oz)
150 ml / 5 fl oz of Almond Milk (Unsweetened)

Protein 5g, Fat 3g, Carb 9g, Fibre 11g, 108 Kcals

Preparation

Put all the solid ingredients into the Tall Cup and press them down below the Max Line. Add the fluid base to fill the cup up to the Max Line. Screw the Nutribullet Extractor Blade on to the top of the cup. Invert the cup, press it down into the Nutribullet Power Base and twist it into place. Blast the mixture until it is really smooth (20 or so seconds). **Enjoy!**

Lettuce and Grapefruit Splash

Ingredients

1 Cup/Handful of Spinach (40 grams or 1½ oz)
1 Cup/Handful of Lettuce Leaves (40 grams or 1½ oz)
½ Cup of Grapefruit segments (60 grams or 2 oz)
1 Cup/Handful of sliced Cauliflower florets (120 grams or 4 oz)
150 ml / 5 fl oz of Almond Milk (Unsweetened)

Protein 5g, Fat 2g, Carb 9g, Fibre 5g, 84 Kcals

Preparation

Put all the solid ingredients into the Tall Cup and press them down below the Max Line. Add the fluid base to fill the cup up to the Max Line. Screw the Nutribullet Extractor Blade on to the top of the cup. Invert the cup, press it down into the Nutribullet Power Base and twist it into place. Blast the mixture until it is really smooth (20 or so seconds). **Enjoy!**

Verdant Fix

Ingredients

1 Cup/Handful of Spinach (40 grams or 1½ oz)
1 Cup/Handful of Rocket/Arugura Lettuce (40 grams or 1½ oz)
½ Cup of Avocado slices (60 grams or 2 oz)
1 Cup/Handful of sliced Zucchini/Courgette (120 grams or 4 oz)
75 ml / 2½ fl oz of Almond Milk (Unsweetened)
75 ml / 2½ fl oz of Greek Yoghurt

Protein 8g, Fat 17g, Carb 9g, Fibre 7g, 235 Kcals

Preparation

Put all the solid ingredients into the Tall Cup and press them down below the Max Line. Add the fluid base to fill the cup up to the Max Line. Screw the Nutribullet Extractor Blade on to the top of the cup. Invert the cup, press it down into the Nutribullet Power Base and twist it into place. Blast the mixture until it is really smooth (20 or so seconds). **Enjoy!**

Fruity Cornucopia

Ingredients

1 Cup/Handful of Spinach (40 grams or 1½ oz)
1 Cup/Handful of Rocket/Arugura Lettuce (40 grams or 1½ oz)
½ Cup of Grapefruit segments (60 grams or 2 oz)
1 Cup/Handful of sliced Green Pepper (120 grams or 4 oz)
150 ml / 5 fl oz of Almond Milk (Unsweetened)

Protein 4g, Fat 2g, Carb 9g, Fibre 5g, 77 Kcals

Preparation

Put all the solid ingredients into the Tall Cup and press them down below the Max Line. Add the fluid base to fill the cup up to the Max Line. Screw the Nutribullet Extractor Blade on to the top of the cup. Invert the cup, press it down into the Nutribullet Power Base and twist it into place. Blast the mixture until it is really smooth (20 or so seconds). **Enjoy!**

Green Melody

Ingredients

2 Cups/Handfuls of Black Kale de-stemmed (80 grams or 3 oz)
½ Cup of Avocado slices (60 grams or 2 oz)
1 Cup/Handful of sliced Zucchini/Courgette (120 grams or 4 oz)
150 ml / 5 fl oz of Coconut Milk

Protein 6g, Fat 12g, Carb 9g, Fibre 7g, 174 Kcals

Preparation

Put all the solid ingredients into the Tall Cup and press them down below the Max Line. Add the fluid base to fill the cup up to the Max Line. Screw the Nutribullet Extractor Blade on to the top of the cup. Invert the cup, press it down into the Nutribullet Power Base and twist it into place. Blast the mixture until it is really smooth (20 or so seconds). **Enjoy!**

Plum loves Asparagus

Ingredients

1 Cup/Handful of Lettuce Leaves (40 grams or 1½ oz)
1 Cup/Handful of Watercress (40 grams or 1½ oz)
½ Cup of Plum halves (60 grams or 2 oz)
1 Cup/Handful of sliced Asparagus (120 grams or 4 oz)
150 ml / 5 fl oz of Almond Milk (Unsweetened)

Protein 5g, Fat 2g, Carb 9g, Fibre 5g, 82 Kcals

Preparation

Put all the solid ingredients into the Tall Cup and press them down below the Max Line. Add the fluid base to fill the cup up to the Max Line. Screw the Nutribullet Extractor Blade on to the top of the cup. Invert the cup, press it down into the Nutribullet Power Base and twist it into place. Blast the mixture until it is really smooth (20 or so seconds). **Enjoy!**

Turnip Tonic

Ingredients

1 Cup/Handful of Bok Choy (40 grams or 1½ oz)
1 Cup/Handful of Rocket/Arugura Lettuce (40 grams or 1½ oz)
½ Cup of Blackberries (60 grams or 2 oz)
1 Cup/Handful of diced Turnip (120 grams or 4 oz)
150 ml / 5 fl oz of Almond Milk (Unsweetened)

Protein 4g, Fat 2g, Carb 9g, Fibre 7g, 90 Kcals

Preparation

Put all the solid ingredients into the Tall Cup and press them down below the Max Line. Add the fluid base to fill the cup up to the Max Line. Screw the Nutribullet Extractor Blade on to the top of the cup. Invert the cup, press it down into the Nutribullet Power Base and twist it into place. Blast the mixture until it is really smooth (20 or so seconds). **Enjoy!**

Fruity Swirl

Ingredients

1 Cup/Handful of Bok Choy (40 grams or 1½ oz)
1 Cup/Handful of Broccoli Florets (40 grams or 1½ oz)
½ Cup of Avocado slices (60 grams or 2 oz)
1 Cup/Handful of sliced Cucumber (120 grams or 4 oz)
150 ml / 5 fl oz of Hazelnut Milk

Protein 4g, Fat 12g, Carb 9g, Fibre 7g, 172 Kcals

Preparation

Put all the solid ingredients into the Tall Cup and press them down below the Max Line. Add the fluid base to fill the cup up to the Max Line. Screw the Nutribullet Extractor Blade on to the top of the cup. Invert the cup, press it down into the Nutribullet Power Base and twist it into place. Blast the mixture until it is really smooth (20 or so seconds). **Enjoy!**

Pineapple Piazza

Ingredients

1 Cup/Handful of Lettuce Leaves (40 grams or 1½ oz)
1 Cup/Handful of Black Kale de-stemmed (40 grams or 1½ oz)
½ Cup of Pineapple chunks (60 grams or 2 oz)
1 Cup/Handful of sliced Celery (120 grams or 4 oz)
150 ml / 5 fl oz of Almond Milk (Unsweetened)

Protein 4g, Fat 3g, Carb 10g, Fibre 5g, 89 Kcals

Preparation

Put all the solid ingredients into the Tall Cup and press them down below the Max Line. Add the fluid base to fill the cup up to the Max Line. Screw the Nutribullet Extractor Blade on to the top of the cup. Invert the cup, press it down into the Nutribullet Power Base and twist it into place. Blast the mixture until it is really smooth (20 or so seconds). **Enjoy!**

Green Waterfall

Ingredients

1 Cup/Handful of Spinach (40 grams or 1½ oz)
1 Cup/Handful of Lettuce Leaves (40 grams or 1½ oz)
½ Cup of Avocado slices (60 grams or 2 oz)
1 Cup/Handful of sliced Cucumber (120 grams or 4 oz)
75 ml / 2½ fl oz of Coconut Milk
75 ml / 2½ fl oz of Greek Yoghurt

Protein 7g, Fat 17g, Carb 10g, Fibre 7g, 235 Kcals

Preparation

Put all the solid ingredients into the Tall Cup and press them down below the Max Line. Add the fluid base to fill the cup up to the Max Line. Screw the Nutribullet Extractor Blade on to the top of the cup. Invert the cup, press it down into the Nutribullet Power Base and twist it into place. Blast the mixture until it is really smooth (20 or so seconds). **Enjoy!**

Verdant Panache

Ingredients

1 Cup/Handful of Red or White Cabbage (40 grams or 1½ oz)
1 Cup/Handful of Green Cabbage (40 grams or 1½ oz)
½ Cup of Raspberries (60 grams or 2 oz)
1 Cup/Handful of sliced Tomato (120 grams or 4 oz)
150 ml / 5 fl oz of Almond Milk (Unsweetened)

Protein 3g, Fat 2g, Carb 10g, Fibre 8g, 94 Kcals

Preparation

Put all the solid ingredients into the Tall Cup and press them down below the Max Line. Add the fluid base to fill the cup up to the Max Line. Screw the Nutribullet Extractor Blade on to the top of the cup. Invert the cup, press it down into the Nutribullet Power Base and twist it into place. Blast the mixture until it is really smooth (20 or so seconds). **Enjoy!**

Red Cabbage goes Broccoli

Ingredients

1 Cup/Handful of Red or White Cabbage (40 grams or 1½ oz)
1 Cup/Handful of Broccoli Florets (40 grams or 1½ oz)
½ Cup of Cranberries (60 grams or 2 oz)
1 Cup/Handful of sliced Celery (120 grams or 4 oz)
150 ml / 5 fl oz of Almond Milk (Unsweetened)

Protein 3g, Fat 2g, Carb 10g, Fibre 7g, 92 Kcals

Preparation

Put all the solid ingredients into the Tall Cup and press them down below the Max Line. Add the fluid base to fill the cup up to the Max Line. Screw the Nutribullet Extractor Blade on to the top of the cup. Invert the cup, press it down into the Nutribullet Power Base and twist it into place. Blast the mixture until it is really smooth (20 or so seconds). **Enjoy!**

Veggie Consortium

Ingredients

2 Cups/Handfuls of Rocket/Arugura Lettuce (80 grams or 3 oz)
½ Cup of Papaya (60 grams or 2 oz)
1 Cup/Handful of sliced Tomato (120 grams or 4 oz)
150 ml / 5 fl oz of Almond Milk (Unsweetened)

Protein 3g, Fat 2g, Carb 10g, Fibre 4g, 78 Kcals

Preparation

Put all the solid ingredients into the Tall Cup and press them down below the Max Line. Add the fluid base to fill the cup up to the Max Line. Screw the Nutribullet Extractor Blade on to the top of the cup. Invert the cup, press it down into the Nutribullet Power Base and twist it into place. Blast the mixture until it is really smooth (20 or so seconds). **Enjoy!**

Lettuce and Watercress Ensemble

Ingredients

1 Cup/Handful of Lettuce Leaves (40 grams or 1½ oz)
1 Cup/Handful of Watercress (40 grams or 1½ oz)
½ Cup of Kiwi Fruit slices (60 grams or 2 oz)
1 Cup/Handful of Radishes (120 grams or 4 oz)
150 ml / 5 fl oz of Almond Milk (Unsweetened)

Protein 4g, Fat 2g, Carb 10g, Fibre 5g, 86 Kcals

Preparation

Put all the solid ingredients into the Tall Cup and press them down below the Max Line. Add the fluid base to fill the cup up to the Max Line. Screw the Nutribullet Extractor Blade on to the top of the cup. Invert the cup, press it down into the Nutribullet Power Base and twist it into place. Blast the mixture until it is really smooth (20 or so seconds). **Enjoy!**

Green Rush

Ingredients

1 Cup/Handful of Mint (40 grams or 1½ oz)
1 Cup/Handful of Rocket/Arugura Lettuce (40 grams or 1½ oz)
½ Cup of Orange segments (60 grams or 2 oz)
1 Cup/Handful of sliced Tomato (120 grams or 4 oz)
150 ml / 5 fl oz of Almond Milk (Unsweetened)

Protein 4g, Fat 2g, Carb 10g, Fibre 7g, 92 Kcals

Preparation

Put all the solid ingredients into the Tall Cup and press them down below the Max Line. Add the fluid base to fill the cup up to the Max Line. Screw the Nutribullet Extractor Blade on to the top of the cup. Invert the cup, press it down into the Nutribullet Power Base and twist it into place. Blast the mixture until it is really smooth (20 or so seconds). **Enjoy!**

Green Infusion

Ingredients

2 Cups/Handfuls of Rocket/Arugura Lettuce (80 grams or 3 oz)
½ Cup of Papaya (60 grams or 2 oz)
1 Cup/Handful of sliced Green Pepper (120 grams or 4 oz)
150 ml / 5 fl oz of Almond Milk (Unsweetened)

Protein 3g, Fat 2g, Carb 10g, Fibre 5g, 81 Kcals

Preparation

Put all the solid ingredients into the Tall Cup and press them down below the Max Line. Add the fluid base to fill the cup up to the Max Line. Screw the Nutribullet Extractor Blade on to the top of the cup. Invert the cup, press it down into the Nutribullet Power Base and twist it into place. Blast the mixture until it is really smooth (20 or so seconds). **Enjoy!**

Blueberry and Asparagus Surprise

Ingredients

1 Cup/Handful of Watercress (40 grams or 1½ oz)
1 Cup/Handful of Lettuce Leaves (40 grams or 1½ oz)
½ Cup of Blueberries (60 grams or 2 oz)
1 Cup/Handful of sliced Asparagus (120 grams or 4 oz)
150 ml / 5 fl oz of Almond Milk (Unsweetened)

Protein 5g, Fat 2g, Carb 10g, Fibre 5g, 88 Kcals

Preparation

Put all the solid ingredients into the Tall Cup and press them down below the Max Line. Add the fluid base to fill the cup up to the Max Line. Screw the Nutribullet Extractor Blade on to the top of the cup. Invert the cup, press it down into the Nutribullet Power Base and twist it into place. Blast the mixture until it is really smooth (20 or so seconds). **Enjoy!**

Green Forever

Ingredients

2 Cups/Handfuls of Green Cabbage (80 grams or 3 oz)
½ Cup of Avocado slices (60 grams or 2 oz)
1 Cup/Handful of sliced Zucchini/Courgette (120 grams or 4 oz)
75 ml / 2½ fl oz of Almond Milk (Unsweetened)
75 ml / 2½ fl oz of Greek Yoghurt

Protein 7g, Fat 17g, Carb 10g, Fibre 8g, 239 Kcals

Preparation

Put all the solid ingredients into the Tall Cup and press them down below the Max Line. Add the fluid base to fill the cup up to the Max Line. Screw the Nutribullet Extractor Blade on to the top of the cup. Invert the cup, press it down into the Nutribullet Power Base and twist it into place. Blast the mixture until it is really smooth (20 or so seconds). **Enjoy!**

Guava meets Celery

Ingredients

2 Cups/Handfuls of Fennel (80 grams or 3 oz)
½ Cup of Guava (60 grams or 2 oz)
1 Cup/Handful of sliced Celery (120 grams or 4 oz)
150 ml / 5 fl oz of Almond Milk (Unsweetened)

Protein 4g, Fat 3g, Carb 10g, Fibre 8g, 104 Kcals

Preparation

Put all the solid ingredients into the Tall Cup and press them down below the Max Line. Add the fluid base to fill the cup up to the Max Line. Screw the Nutribullet Extractor Blade on to the top of the cup. Invert the cup, press it down into the Nutribullet Power Base and twist it into place. Blast the mixture until it is really smooth (20 or so seconds). **Enjoy!**

Spinach in Strawberry

Ingredients

2 Cups/Handfuls of Spinach (80 grams or 3 oz)
½ Cup of Strawberries (60 grams or 2 oz)
1 Cup/Handful of sliced Cucumber (120 grams or 4 oz)
75 ml / 2½ fl oz of Almond Milk (Unsweetened)
75 ml / 2½ fl oz of Greek Yoghurt

Protein 7g, Fat 9g, Carb 11g, Fibre 4g, 155 Kcals

Preparation

Put all the solid ingredients into the Tall Cup and press them down below the Max Line. Add the fluid base to fill the cup up to the Max Line. Screw the Nutribullet Extractor Blade on to the top of the cup. Invert the cup, press it down into the Nutribullet Power Base and twist it into place. Blast the mixture until it is really smooth (20 or so seconds). **Enjoy!**

Mint needs Lettuce

Ingredients

1 Cup/Handful of Mint (40 grams or 1½ oz)
1 Cup/Handful of Lettuce Leaves (40 grams or 1½ oz)
½ Cup of Raspberries (60 grams or 2 oz)
1 Cup/Handful of sliced Celery (120 grams or 4 oz)
150 ml / 5 fl oz of Hazelnut Milk

Protein 4g, Fat 3g, Carb 11g, Fibre 10g, 118 Kcals

Preparation

Put all the solid ingredients into the Tall Cup and press them down below the Max Line. Add the fluid base to fill the cup up to the Max Line. Screw the Nutribullet Extractor Blade on to the top of the cup. Invert the cup, press it down into the Nutribullet Power Base and twist it into place. Blast the mixture until it is really smooth (20 or so seconds). **Enjoy!**

Watercress embraces Black Kale

Ingredients

1 Cup/Handful of Watercress (40 grams or 1½ oz)
1 Cup/Handful of Black Kale de-stemmed (40 grams or 1½ oz)
½ Cup of Avocado slices (60 grams or 2 oz)
1 Cup/Handful of sliced Asparagus (120 grams or 4 oz)
75 ml / 2½ fl oz of Coconut Milk
75 ml / 2½ fl oz of Greek Yoghurt

Protein 9g, Fat 17g, Carb 11g, Fibre 8g, 247 Kcals

Preparation

Put all the solid ingredients into the Tall Cup and press them down below the Max Line. Add the fluid base to fill the cup up to the Max Line. Screw the Nutribullet Extractor Blade on to the top of the cup. Invert the cup, press it down into the Nutribullet Power Base and twist it into place. Blast the mixture until it is really smooth (20 or so seconds). **Enjoy!**

Veggie Miracle

Ingredients

1 Cup/Handful of Rocket/Arugura Lettuce (40 grams or 1½ oz)
1 Cup/Handful of Red or White Cabbage (40 grams or 1½ oz)
½ Cup of Avocado slices (60 grams or 2 oz)
1 Cup/Handful of sliced Asparagus (120 grams or 4 oz)
150 ml / 5 fl oz of Hazelnut Milk

Protein 5g, Fat 11g, Carb 11g, Fibre 8g, 181 Kcals

Preparation

Put all the solid ingredients into the Tall Cup and press them down below the Max Line. Add the fluid base to fill the cup up to the Max Line. Screw the Nutribullet Extractor Blade on to the top of the cup. Invert the cup, press it down into the Nutribullet Power Base and twist it into place. Blast the mixture until it is really smooth (20 or so seconds). **Enjoy!**

Blueberry Blockbuster

Ingredients

2 Cups/Handfuls of Bok Choy (80 grams or 3 oz)
½ Cup of Blueberries (60 grams or 2 oz)
1 Cup/Handful of sliced Asparagus (120 grams or 4 oz)
150 ml / 5 fl oz of Almond Milk (Unsweetened)

Protein 5g, Fat 2g, Carb 11g, Fibre 5g, 88 Kcals

Preparation

Put all the solid ingredients into the Tall Cup and press them down below the Max Line. Add the fluid base to fill the cup up to the Max Line. Screw the Nutribullet Extractor Blade on to the top of the cup. Invert the cup, press it down into the Nutribullet Power Base and twist it into place. Blast the mixture until it is really smooth (20 or so seconds). **Enjoy!**

Green Cabbage joins Watercress

Ingredients

1 Cup/Handful of Green Cabbage (40 grams or 1½ oz)
1 Cup/Handful of Watercress (40 grams or 1½ oz)
½ Cup of Avocado slices (60 grams or 2 oz)
1 Cup/Handful of sliced Fine Beans (120 grams or 4 oz)
150 ml / 5 fl oz of Coconut Milk

Protein 5g, Fat 11g, Carb 11g, Fibre 8g, 170 Kcals

Preparation

Put all the solid ingredients into the Tall Cup and press them down below the Max Line. Add the fluid base to fill the cup up to the Max Line. Screw the Nutribullet Extractor Blade on to the top of the cup. Invert the cup, press it down into the Nutribullet Power Base and twist it into place. Blast the mixture until it is really smooth (20 or so seconds). **Enjoy!**

Orange and Radish Bliss

Ingredients

1 Cup/Handful of Red or White Cabbage (40 grams or 1½ oz)
1 Cup/Handful of Mint (40 grams or 1½ oz)
½ Cup of Orange segments (60 grams or 2 oz)
1 Cup/Handful of Radishes (120 grams or 4 oz)
150 ml / 5 fl oz of Almond Milk (Unsweetened)

Protein 4g, Fat 2g, Carb 11g, Fibre 8g, 96 Kcals

Preparation

Put all the solid ingredients into the Tall Cup and press them down below the Max Line. Add the fluid base to fill the cup up to the Max Line. Screw the Nutribullet Extractor Blade on to the top of the cup. Invert the cup, press it down into the Nutribullet Power Base and twist it into place. Blast the mixture until it is really smooth (20 or so seconds). **Enjoy!**

Green Cabbage and Red Cabbage Splendour

Ingredients

1 Cup/Handful of Green Cabbage (40 grams or 1½ oz)
1 Cup/Handful of Red or White Cabbage (40 grams or 1½ oz)
½ Cup of Papaya (60 grams or 2 oz)
1 Cup/Handful of sliced Cucumber (120 grams or 4 oz)
150 ml / 5 fl oz of Almond Milk (Unsweetened)

Protein 3g, Fat 2g, Carb 11g, Fibre 4g, 82 Kcals

Preparation

Put all the solid ingredients into the Tall Cup and press them down below the Max Line. Add the fluid base to fill the cup up to the Max Line. Screw the Nutribullet Extractor Blade on to the top of the cup. Invert the cup, press it down into the Nutribullet Power Base and twist it into place. Blast the mixture until it is really smooth (20 or so seconds). **Enjoy!**

Strawberry on Swede

Ingredients

1 Cup/Handful of Black Kale de-stemmed (40 grams or 1½ oz)
1 Cup/Handful of Spinach (40 grams or 1½ oz)
½ Cup of Strawberries (60 grams or 2 oz)
1 Cup/Handful of diced Swede (120 grams or 4 oz)
150 ml / 5 fl oz of Almond Milk (Unsweetened)

Protein 4g, Fat 3g, Carb 11g, Fibre 6g, 96 Kcals

Preparation

Put all the solid ingredients into the Tall Cup and press them down below the Max Line. Add the fluid base to fill the cup up to the Max Line. Screw the Nutribullet Extractor Blade on to the top of the cup. Invert the cup, press it down into the Nutribullet Power Base and twist it into place. Blast the mixture until it is really smooth (20 or so seconds). **Enjoy!**

NOTES

NOTES

64065640R00071

Made in the USA
Lexington, KY
26 May 2017